THE COMPLETE
SLOW COOKER

THE COMPLETE
SLOW COOKER

PACKED WITH RECIPES, TECHNIQUES AND TIPS

Sara Lewis

Bounty
Books

This edition published in 2014 by Bounty Books
a division of Octopus Publishing Group Ltd
Carmelite House, 50 Victoria Embankment
London EC4Y 0DZ
www.octopusbooks.co.uk

An Hachette UK Company
www.hachette.co.uk

First published in Great Britain in 2010 by Hamlyn, a
division of Octopus Publishing Group Ltd

Sara Lewis asserts the moral right to be identified as the
author of this work.

ISBN 978-0-753728-54-3

A CIP catalogue record for this book is available from
the British Library

Printed and bound in China

Standard level spoon measures are used in all recipes:
1 tablespoon = one 15 ml spoon
1 teaspoon = one 5 ml spoon

Both metric and imperial measurements are given for the
recipes. Use one set of measures only, not a mixture of both.
Medium eggs have been used throughout.
Fresh herbs should be used unless otherwise stated.
A few recipes contain nuts and nut derivatives. Anyone with
a known nut allergy must avoid these.
This book contains some dishes made with raw or lightly
cooked eggs. It is prudent for more vulnerable people such as
pregnant and nursing mothers, invalids, the elderly, babies and
young children to avoid raw or lightly cooked eggs.
Read your slow cooker manual before you begin and preheat
the slow cooker if required according to the manufacturer's
instructions. Because slow cookers vary slightly from
manufacturer to manufacturer, check recipe timings with the
manufacturer's directions for a recipe using the same ingredients.
All recipes for this book were tested in oval-shaped slow cookers
with a working capacity of 2.5 litres (4 pints) and total capacity
of 3.5 litres (6 pints) using metric measurements. Where the slow
cooker recipe is finished off under the grill, hold the pot with
teacloths to remove it from the machine housing.

Contents

Introduction

If you've just bought your first slow cooker, congratulations. You're going to enjoy plenty of delicious and succulent meals. Before you use your cooker for the first time, however, read this introduction so that you get the best from it.

Slow cooking

If you were brought up by a parent who was a believer in slow cooking – and who probably still has their first slow cooker, which could now be over 30 years old and still going strong – then you'll appreciate what it was like to come home to a properly cooked supper.

Now you can do the same for yourself and your family no matter how pushed for time you are or how late you are working in the evening. Slow-cooked dishes are back in vogue once again, and cuts of meat, such as slow-cooked pork, which several years ago would have been laughed at, are now appearing on the menus of many a smart gastropub. From pot-roasts and preserves to braised oxtail and one-pot dinners, timeless classic family meals are more popular than ever. More importantly, these are the kind of dishes that can easily and simply be prepared at home, and a slow cooker has become an essential kitchen utensil for the 21st century.

The appeal of slow cookers

What is the slow cooker phenomenon all about? The main appeal is that it cooks food so slowly that the food doesn't boil dry and can be left unattended for 8–10 hours without any danger that it will boil over or burn on the bottom of the pan. That said, some ingredients do need to be fried first, but then you simply add everything to the slow cooker and get on with the rest of the day.

If the convenience isn't enough to persuade you, then you will find that the flavour you can achieve is second to none. Meaty casseroles or dishes infused with spices and herbs seem to melt in the mouth. You can also save money by using less well known, cheaper cuts of meat, such as neck of lamb, rabbit and bacon hocks, and even Sunday lunch – half a shoulder of lamb, a braised brisket of beef or a pot-roast chicken – can be easily prepared in a slow cooker.

Not only is a slow cooker easy to use, but it will enhance the flavour of your food and is cheap to run (costing about the same price as a lightbulb), thereby saving fuel, which is good for the environment.

Saving time

Although the idea of getting supper ready before you go out in the morning may seem like the last thing you want to do or can fit in, once you have tried it a few times, you will be won round. Spending just 15–20 minutes early in the day will enable you to prepare supper in your slow cooker, leaving you time to get on with something else. If you have a young family, supper can be put on after the morning school run so that it is ready when you and the children are at your most exhausted in the late afternoon. If you are working shifts or if you are a student with a busy day of lectures, you could put on a meal before you go out so that a hot supper is waiting when you get back home. If you are new to retirement, supper can be left to cook while you enjoy a relaxing day playing golf or tackling a DIY project.

How to use this book

This book will guide you through the range of dishes you can make with a slow cooker, helping you understand how to get the most out of this versatile cooking tool. There are recipes for everyday favourites as well as for dishes to share with friends, such as Salmon-wrapped Cod with Buttered Leeks (see pages 176–177) or Venison Puff Pie (see pages 170–171). There are also plenty of vegetarian treats, such as Aubergine Ratatouille with Ricotta Dumplings (see pages 142–143) and Balsamic Tomatoes with Spaghetti (see pages 148–149).

As well as basic safety and start-up advice, there is also advice on different ways to use a slow cooker and how it can change your cooking lifestyle. To make puddings such as Christmas Pudding (see pages 212–213) you can simply put a pudding basin directly on to the base of the slow cooker pot and add water. You can also use a slow cooker as a bain marie or water bath to cook baked custards, pâtés and terrines. Pour mixtures of alcohol and fruit juice into the pot and heat them up to make warming hot party punches or hot toddies, which can be ladled out as required. You will find that you can easily make a wide variety of dishes such as chocolate or cheese fondues, preserves and simple chutneys, or even boil up the bones or a chicken carcass to make homemade stock.

There is also a chapter of recipes for short-cut suppers (see pages 98–119), which don't involve browning the meat beforehand, and, if you are really short of time, there is a chapter of cheat's recipes (see pages 232–251) that make good use of ready-made jars, cans and chilled extras.

A new lifestyle

Although your friends might tease you about how long your casseroles have been in the oven, once you have experienced the advantages of using a slow cooker you will find that it suits your way of life. You might even find that you will take your slow cooker on self-catering holidays: after a busy day on the beach or sight-seeing, there are few things more welcoming than the aroma of supper bubbling away. Slow cookers don't just mean winter stews, as the recipe for Smoked Cod with Cannellini Bean Mash (see pages 104–105) proves.

Whatever your circumstances, slow cooking can be a lifesaver. They are environmentally friendly, cheap to run, won't boil dry and are incredibly versatile – everyone should have one. So, put the meal on, take the dog out for a walk, put the children to bed or have a glass of wine in the garden ... and supper is ready when you are.

Slow cooker basics

Choosing a slow cooker

The best and most versatile slow cookers are oval in shape. They are ideal for cooking a whole chicken, have ample room for a pudding basin or four individual pudding moulds and are capacious enough to make soup for six people.

Slow cookers are available in three sizes and are measured in total capacity; the size is usually printed on the packaging with the working capacity or the maximum space for food:

* for two people choose a mini oval slow cooker with a maximum capacity of 1.5 litres (2½ pints) and a working capacity of 1 litre (1¾ pints)
* for four people choose either a round or a more versatile oval cooker with a total capacity of 3.5 litres (6 pints) and a working capacity of 2.5 litres (4 pints)
* for six people choose a large, oval slow cooker with a total capacity of 5 litres (8¾ pints) and a working capacity of 4 litres (7 pints) or the extra large, round 6.5 litre (11½ pint) cooker with a working capacity of 4.5 litres (8 pints).

Perhaps surprisingly, the very large slow cookers cost only a little more than the medium-size models, and so it is easy to be swept along thinking that they are better value for money. Unless you have a large family or like

to cook large quantities so that you have enough supper for one meal with extra portions to freeze, you will probably find that they are too big for your everyday needs. Remember that you need to half-fill a slow cooker when cooking meat, fish or vegetable dishes.

Before you begin

Although it might seem obvious, always check that the joint, pudding basin, soufflé dish or individual moulds will fit into your slow cooker pot before you begin, to avoid frustration when you are halfway through making a recipe.

PREHEATING

It is important that you read the manual or handbook that came with your slow cooker before you begin cooking. Some manufacturers recommend preheating the slow cooker on the high setting for a minimum of 20 minutes before food is added. The majority however, recommend that the slow cooker is heated only when it has been filled with food.

Changing recipes for a different cooker size

All the recipes in this book have been tested in a standard sized slow cooker with a total capacity of 3.5 litres (6 pints). If you have a 5 litre (8¾ pint) six-portion cookers or a 1.5 litre (2½ pint) two-person cooker you can adapt the recipes in this book by simply halving the ingredients for two portions or adding half as much again to the recipe for six, keeping the timings the same. All the recipes made in a pudding basin, soufflé dish or individual moulds may also be cooked in a larger slow cooker for the same length of time.

SAFETY FIRST

Before you start to use the slow cooker put it on the work surface, somewhere out of the way, and make sure that the flex is tucked around the back of the machine and not trailing over the front of the work surface or near the hob.

The outside of the slow cooker does get hot, so wear oven gloves when you lift the pot out of the housing to serve. Set it on to a heatproof mat on the table or work surface to serve the food. If the slow cooker lid has a vent in the top, make sure that the cooker is not placed under an eye-level cupboard or the steam might catch someone's arm as they reach into the cupboard.

Never reheat cooked food in a slow cooker. Heat up a cooked casserole in a saucepan on the hob and make sure to bring it to the boil and cook it through thoroughly. Only reheat cooked food once.

Slow cooker techniques

Basic frying preparation

There are two basic approaches. You can fry the meat, then add onions and flavourings. Stir in flour at this point, then add stock and flavourings. Bring the mixture to the boil, then spoon it into the slow cooker pot.

This method arguably gives the best flavour and colour, but the idea of frying meat and onions first thing in the morning can be a bit off-putting, and if you prefer you can prepare all the ingredients the night before. Mix ingredients such as flavourings in a bowl, cover with clingfilm and chill in the refrigerator. Don't be tempted to part-fry meat and chill it. In the morning add the ingredients to the slow cooker pot without frying anything first, and then add hot liquid, heated in the microwave, in a saucepan or by crumbling a stock cube into a jug and mixing with boiling water. Depending on the recipe, you might want to increase the cooking time by 1–2 hours.

Liquid is key

A slow cooker is really like a large insulated saucepan, and although it must never be used without added liquid, the amount needed is less than when you are simmering a pan on the hob for several hours because there is no danger that it will boil dry. As the casserole

heats up, the liquid turns to steam, which condenses on the lid and falls back into the pot, which is the reason why you need less stock. Because the heat is constant you can safely leave the machine on even when you are not in the house.

Filling the pot

When you buy a slow cooker you will find, confusingly, that the manufacturer has put two figures on the side of the box. The lower figure is the space for cooking, and the higher figure is the total capacity of the slow cooker pot.

Aim to fill the slow cooker pot between half and three-quarters full. Joints of meat should fill no more than two-thirds of the pot. If you are using a pudding basin or ovenproof dish allow 1 cm (½ inch) at the narrowest point in an oval pot or 2 cm (¾ inch) in a round one. If you are making soup the pot can be a little fuller, but make sure that the liquid level is no higher than 2.5 cm (1 inch) from the top.

Heat settings

All slow cookers have a 'high', 'low' and 'off' setting, and some models also have either 'medium', 'warm' or 'auto' settings. In general, the high setting will take only half the time of the low setting when you are cooking a casserole containing diced meat or vegetables. This can be useful if you plan to eat at lunchtime or get delayed in starting the casserole. Both settings will reach just below 100°C (212°F) or boiling point during cooking, but when set to 'high' the temperature is reached more quickly.

An auto setting, although not crucial, is helpful if you plan to add meat without frying it first because it starts the slow cooker on high then automatically reduces the heat to low by means of a thermostat. The auto setting is also useful if the slow cooker is very full. If you don't have this facility start the recipe on high for 30 minutes, then reduce the heat manually before you leave the house.

Increasing the temperature from low to high at the end of a recipe can be useful if you want to thicken the casserole with cornflour at the end of cooking, add extra green vegetables or reheat soups that have been puréed and then returned to the slow cooker pot.

The warm setting is suitable once the maximum cooking time is reached, to keep the food on hold, which is convenient for late diners but not essential, because the low setting will not cause foods to spoil unless they are rice based.

Cooking times

The slow cooker will help you to make the most of your time. The table below shows how long different types of food, and some recipes in this book, take in the slow cooker, and at what setting, so that you can plan your time in and out of the kitchen. These timings show how long the food takes to cook in the slow cooker. Initial preparation and final touches such as browning under the grill and preparing accompaniments are not included.

Cook on low

1–2 hours
Poached halved bananas, apple wedges or halved peaches, Chocolate Puddings (pages 192–193)

2–3 hours
Fish soups, fruit compotes, rice pudding made with risotto rice rather than pudding rice, Crème Caramels (pages 194–195), Honeyed Rice Pudding (page 198)

3–4 hours
Squid, poached pear halves, individual crème brûlées, lemon curd, Mackerel Kedgeree (pages 94–95)

4–5 hours
Cheesy macaroni, vegetable soups without potatoes, stuffed peppers, bread and butter pudding, Tuna Arrabiata (pages 84–85)

6–8 hours
Sausages, diced boneless chicken and boneless chicken breasts, soups with diced potato, vegetable stews, curries and gnocchi, meatballs, Barley Risotto with Blue Cheese Butter (pages 100–101)

8–10 hours
Casseroles or soups with diced meat, beef and lamb mince, sliced lamb fillet, whole lamb rump steaks or chump chops, pork shoulder steaks or boneless spare rib pork chops, chicken thighs and drumsticks on the bone, oxtail, bean stews, marmalade base

Cook on high

Under 1 hour
Cheese or chocolate fondue, Eggs en Cocotte with Smoked Salmon (pages 40–41)

1–2 hours
Porridge, soused herrings, whole trout, 500 g (1 lb) thick piece salmon fillet, Courgette & Broad Bean Frittata (pages 48–49), Aubergine Timbale (pages 158–159)

2–3 hours
Sweetcorn chilli, kidneys, braised red cabbage or diced beetroot, cheesecake, fruit jellies and conserves, individual sponge puddings, Mediterranean Roasted Vegetable Terrine (pages 52–53)

3–4 hours
Whole boneless chicken breasts, 500 g (1 lb) haggis, 750 g (1 1/2 lb) whole pheasant, lentil dhal, tomato pasta sauce, 1.2–1.5 litre (2–2 1/2 pint) steamed sponge pudding, Aubergine Ratatouille with Ricotta Dumplings (pages 142–143)

4–5 hours
Spanish baked potatoes, braised celery, Lemon & Poppy Seed Drizzle Cake (pages 210–211)

5–6 hours
Pork ribs, lamb shanks, duck legs, rilettes, meatloaf and pâté, ox tongue, 1.25 litre (2 1/4 pint) steak and kidney pudding, 1 kg (2 lb) whole guinea fowl, 1.5 kg (3 lb) whole chicken, Duck, Pork & Apple Rillettes (pages 54–55)

6–7 hours
1.25 kg (2 1/2 lb) gammon joint, 1 kg (2 lb) pork or ham hock, neck of lamb on the bone, breast of lamb, turkey drumstick, 1 kg (2 lb) beef brisket, chutney

7–8 hours
Hotpot with sliced potato topping, 875 g (1 3/4 lb) piece thick belly pork, half a shoulder of lamb, 1.5 litre (2 1/2 pint) Christmas pudding, Minted Lamb with Beetroot Couscous (pages 178–179)

What to cook at what setting

All the recipes in this book show a span of cooking time, which means the dish will be cooked and ready to eat at the shorter time but can be left without spoiling for an extra hour or so.

Pieces of meat can be cooked on low or high, but larger joints must be cooked on high so that they are cooked right through. If you are not sure how long to cook something, err on the generous side because the heat is so gentle that even food that has been in longer than really necessary will not dry out.

If you are unsure if meat is cooked through cut into the thickest part of the chicken, rabbit, pheasant, guinea fowl or pork: the juices should run clear with no hint of pink. Beef and lamb can be eaten slightly pink so it isn't so crucial for them. Make doubly sure with a meat thermometer if you don't feel confident. Fish should break easily into pieces and the flakes should be the same colour all the way through.

Adjusting the cooking time

If you want to slow down or speed up timings for diced meat or vegetable casseroles so that they fit around your plans better, adjust the heat settings and timings as suggested below:

Cook on low	Cook on medium	Cook on high
6–8 hours	4–6 hours	3–4 hours
8–10 hours	6–8 hours	5–6 hours
10–12 hours	8–10 hours	7–8 hours

Note: These timings were taken from the Morphy Richards slow cooker instruction handbook. Do not change timings or settings for fish, whole joints or dairy dishes in recipes.

Slow cooker ingredients

Meat

To make sure that meat is properly cooked cut it into equal sized pieces so that cooking is even and fry meat before adding to the slow cooker.

A whole guinea fowl or pheasant, even a small gammon joint or half a shoulder of lamb can also be cooked in an oval slow cooker pot, but make sure that it does not fill more than the lower two-thirds of the pot, then cover with boiling liquid and cook on high. Check

that the meat is cooked before serving either by using a meat thermometer or inserting a skewer through the thickest part and checking that the juices run clear.

Add boiling stock or sauce to the slow cooker pot and press the meat beneath the surface of the hot stock before cooking begins.

Vegetables and fruit

Surprisingly, root vegetables can take longer to cook than meat, so make sure that you cut them into small enough pieces. The amount of liquid and size of the vegetable chunks greatly affects the speed of cooking in a slow cooker: the more liquid and the smaller the size of vegetable chunk, the quicker the cooking. Denser root vegetables take almost the same time to cook as diced beef.

If you are adding vegetables to a meaty casserole, make sure that the pieces are a little smaller than the meat, and try to keep all the vegetable chunks the same size so that they cook evenly. Press the vegetables and meat below the surface of the liquid with the back of a spoon before cooking commences.

If you are making soup, purée it while it is still in the slow cooker pot using an electric stick blender if you have one. Or transfer the soup to a freestanding liquidizer or food processor, blend and return to the slow cooker.

Cut potatoes will turn black if they not cooked beneath stock, so make sure that you press them beneath the surface of the stock before cooking. Apples, pears and bananas will also discolour, so toss them in a little lemon juice before cooking.

Slow cooker basics
* Foods cooked in a slow cooker must contain some liquid.
* Foods will not brown during cooking, so fry foods before they go in or brown the top by transferring the slow cooker pot from its housing to the grill just before serving. Alternatively, use a cook's blow torch.
* The smaller the pieces of food the quicker they will cook.
* Food at the bottom of the slow cooker pot will cook more quickly, so put root vegetables into the pot first.

Fish

The slow, gentle cooking means that individual pieces of fish or a larger 500 g (1 b) piece will not break up or overcook. Make sure that the fish is covered by the hot liquid so that it cooks evenly.

Add peeled prawns or shelled mussels to a tomato-based pasta sauce or soup at the end of cooking and cook on high for 20–30 minutes until piping hot.

If you are using frozen fish it must be thoroughly defrosted, rinsed with cold water and drained before cooking. Bags of frozen mixed shellfish which contain sliced squid, shelled mussels and prawns must also be defrosted thoroughly before use.

Lentils and pulses

Canned beans have been used in the recipes in this book because they are quick and convenient, but if you prefer to use dried beans soak them overnight in cold water. Drain them, then tip them into a saucepan and cover with fresh water. Bring to the boil and boil rapidly for 10 minutes. Drain again and add to the slow cooker pot with the other ingredients and cover with hot stock. Cook on high for 6–7 hours.

Pearl barley and red, Puy or green lentils do not need soaking overnight, but if you are not sure check the instructions on the packet. These can be cooked on low.

Rice

Easy-cook rice is preferable for slow cookers because it has been partially cooked during manufacture. Some of the starch has been washed off, making it less sticky when cooked.

Thickening casseroles

Casseroles can be thickened in the same way as if you were cooking conventionally. You can do this before slow cooking, by adding the flour after searing the meat or frying the onions, then gradually mixing in the stock. You can mix cornflour with a little water and stir in the mixture 15–30 minutes (on high) or 30–60 minutes (on low) before the end of cooking. Alternatively, pour off the liquid from the cooked dish into a saucepan or frying pan and boil on the hob to reduce. Because the liquid does not evaporate during cooking as it would on the hob, there is no need to lift the lid and check on the stew's progress or top up with stock during cooking. You will probably find that you can use less stock than you would normally do, but it is important that the meat and vegetables are covered with stock so that they cook evenly.

When you are cooking rice allow a minimum of 250 ml (8 fl oz) water for each 100 g (3½ oz) of easy-cook rice or up to 500 ml (17 fl oz) water for the same quantity of risotto rice. You can make risottos in a slow cooker, but unlike making them in a frying pan, when the warm stock is added ladle by ladle, you will need to add all the stock in one go.

Use risotto rice when you make rice puddings because it cooks more quickly than the more traditional round-grain pudding rice.

Pasta

For best results cook the pasta separately in a saucepan of boiling water and then mix with the casserole just before serving. Small pasta shapes, such as macaroni or shells, can be added to soups 20–30 minutes before the end of cooking, as in Chicken & Noodle Broth (see page 35).

Cream and milk

Use full-fat milk or double cream, which are less likely to separate. Cream and milk are usually added at the beginning of cooking only in rice pudding or baked egg custard-style dishes.

If you are making soup add the milk at the end, when the soup has been puréed. Stir cream into soups just 15 minutes before the end of cooking or swirl over the soup when you have ladled it into soup bowls.

Using ready-made sauces

Simply fry the meat and onions as you would if you were going to cook them in the oven. Add the sauce and bring to the boil, then transfer to the slow cooker pot.

If you prefer not to fry the meat first, put it straight into the slow cooker pot with any vegetables and bring the sauce to the boil in a bowl in the microwave or a saucepan on the hob. Pour the sauce over the meat in the slow cooker and then cook at the setting and for the time recommended in the table on page 13. If the sauce seems a little thick don't be tempted to add more liquid because the juices from the meat will thin it during cooking.

You will need a 400 g (13 oz) jar or can or larger for 4 chops, 4 chicken breasts or 500 g (1 lb) of mince. The sauce must be hot when you add it to the slow cooker. Don't be tempted to add salt to recipes made with bought sauces or soups because these will be seasoned already.

Adapting your own recipes

If you have a favourite recipe, perhaps from a TV chef, one given to you by a friend or handed down within your family, and you feel it would cook perfectly in the slow cooker, then try adapting it.

Look at the table on page 13 and compare the ingredients in your recipe with the same main ingredient. Check with the ingredients list in the manufacturer's handbook, which will indicate the quantity that will fit in the slow cooker pot and the appropriate timing for the main ingredient.

You will probably need to reduce the amount of liquid that the recipes use. However, some slow cooker lids don't seem to fit as well as others, and these models may need topping up with a little extra stock if you are cooking on high. Placing a folded tea towel on top of the lid will help to make a better seal. As with any kind of cooker, you need to get to know your own model.

Adjusting liquid levels

You can add extra flavour to basic recipes with a little wine, some beer or some dry cider. If you are adding lots of fresh tomatoes remember that these will make extra juice as they turn to pulp during cooking.

If you haven't got the liquid levels quite right, add a little hot stock at the end of cooking or when you notice that things look a bit dry. If there is too much sauce at the end, pour it into a saucepan and boil rapidly for 5–10 minutes to reduce it. Or, if you prefer, thicken it with a little cornflour mixed to a paste with some water, stirring this into the slow cooker and cooking on high for 15–30 minutes. Stir again just before serving.

Getting the ingredients right

Remember that any kind of meat or vegetable casserole, stew or curry can be adapted successfully. Find a recipe with a similar main ingredient in the book or your slow cooker handbook so that you can gauge the amount that will fit into the slow cooker pot and help you work out the cooking time.

Cut down the amount of liquid by one-third, possibly even by half if you are using fresh tomatoes, but bear in mind that you must never use the slow cooker without any liquid.

Meat doesn't have to be fried first, but hot stock or sauce must always be added when you are cooking savoury dishes. Remember to cut meat and vegetables into even-sized chunks and make sure that root vegetables are in smaller pieces and that you put them in the bottom of the slow cooker where it is hotter so that they cook faster.

If you use your slow cooker as a water bath for steamed puddings, pâtés, meatloaf or a cake, check that the dish will fit into the slow cooker pot before you begin. There is nothing more frustrating than finding that it won't fit when you have made the recipe and are ready to cook it.

Making the most of your slow cooker

Slow cookers are not just for cooking casseroles and stews for your main meal but are great for preparing a meal at anytime of the day.

Breakfast

Treat yourself to a cooked breakfast if you have a particularly early start or long drive ahead of you. Put breakfast on before you go to bed. Sausage or frankfurter and bean mixtures make good breakfasts, as do dried fruit compotes, which are delicious topped with spoonfuls of yogurt and honey.

You can cook porridge overnight, but mix milk with water because the long cooking causes the milk to denature. Alternatively, use longlife milk, which has been heat treated, and sweeten the porridge just before serving. If you prefer, try Banana & Cinnamon Porridge (see pages 42–43), which can be made in the morning with boiling water. Put it on when you first get up, go for a jog or walk the dog and come back to a healthy breakfast.

Soups

Give your family hearty soups by making homemade chicken stock with the remains of a chicken carcass from the Sunday roast. Strain the liquid, then add rice, pasta, lentils, barley or mixed vegetables. There are no end of appetizing variations. You can purée the soup or leave it chunky if you prefer.

If you are really hungry add mini meatballs or dumplings or drop in a raw egg and leave it until it is cooked through. Top soup with toasted croutons spread with olive tapenade, pesto or a sprinkling of cheese, baked puff pastry shapes or croutons rubbed with a cut garlic clove and fried in olive oil.

Pâtés, potted meat and meatloaf

You can easily make pâtes, potted meat and meatloaf by using the slow cooker as a bain marie or water bath. Check that the dish will fit in your slow cooker before you begin – a round, soufflé-style dish is ideal – line it with bacon and fill with a coarse or fine pâté and bake until firm and the juices run clear. Try Turkey & Cranberry Meatloaf (see pages 56–57) or make Aubergine Timbale (see page 158–159).

Egg custards

Bake delicious individual egg custards and brûlées in a water bath. The gentle heat of the slow cooker gives them a perfect finish. Cover with foil so that the condensation doesn't drip into the custard and bake until just set. For an individual pudding allow $2^1/_2$–$3^1/_2$ hours on low.

Lifting pudding basins

Lift a large basin into the slow cooker by tying string around the edge of the basin and making a string handle. Although this is not crucial when you are adding a cold basin to the slow cooker, it's invaluable when the basin is hot at the end of cooking. Alternatively, use two strips of folded foil, set at right angles to each other, and twist the ends together to make a harness.

Puddings

In winter what could be better than a wonderful sweet or savoury pudding? Line a large pudding basin with suet crust pastry and either fill with sliced sirloin or rump steak and a rich gravy or cook mushrooms and chestnuts in a rich red wine sauce.

For satisfying desserts soak raisins in rum to make a grown-up version of spotted dick or try Sticky Marmalade Syrup Pudding (see pages 200–201).

Preserves

You can create perfect small gifts for friends in your slow cooker by making homemade jams and preserves. Although a slow cooker will not be able to boil a jam rapidly to setting point, it's perfect for the first stage when slowly simmering whole oranges for marmalade or cooking windfall apples, quinces or other orchard fruits for jellies.

You can also make chutneys and softly set fruit conserves, such as Apricot Conserve (see page 224), for which a mix of fresh and dried fruits are cooked together. Although it's not a true jam, the dried fruits swell to give a thick, spreadable jam that stores well in the refrigerator. You can also easily make lemon curd, for which the slow cooker is used rather like a double boiler or water bath, eliminating the danger of overheating and curdling the eggs.

Drinks

While away a cold damp Sunday afternoon with the newspapers, an old film on TV and a glass or two of Hot Buttered Rum (see page 230). If you are hosting a winter party serve a hot drink such as Mulled Wine (see page 227), which can be made in advance and then left to slowly simmer. As guests arrive, remove the lid and allow them to help themselves or refill glasses when needed.

Making the most of casseroles

There are plenty of ways you can make a basic casserole more special or more filling by adding extra toppings towards the end of the cooking time.

MASHED POTATOES

Add a topping of mashed potatoes and a sprinkling of cheese, take the slow cooker pot out of the housing and brown the cheese under the grill. Because the pot is so deep it may not fit under a conventional separate grill, but it will fit into an oven with an integral grill.

DUMPLINGS

Make dumplings with half the quantity of suet to self-raising flour and mix with 1 tablespoon cold water for every 25 g (1 oz) of flour. You can leave dumplings plain or flavour them with chopped herbs, mustard or crushed pepper and lemon rind. Shape them into balls about the size of a walnut, add to the hot casserole and cook on low for about 1 hour or on high for 30–40 minutes until well risen and dry to the touch.

SCONES

Flavour a basic scone recipe with grated Cheddar, Parmesan or crumbled blue cheese or with chopped walnuts, basil, sun-dried tomatoes or black pitted olives. Cut the scone dough into circles or wedges, arrange them on your casserole and cook on high for 45–60 minutes until well risen. Brush with egg before browning under the grill.

PUFF PASTRY

Roll out some ready-rolled puff pastry on a lightly floured surface and cut it into an oval about the size of your slow cooker. Transfer it to a greased baking sheet, brush with beaten egg, then leave it as it is or sprinkle with some torn thyme leaves and coarse sea salt, some sesame seeds or a few crushed fennel seeds. Cook in a preheated oven, 220°C (425°F), Gas Mark 7, for about 15 minutes until well risen and golden. Cut into wedges and serve on top of your casserole.

CHEAT'S TOAD IN THE HOLE

Buy some ready-made Yorkshire puddings, reheat in the oven and fill with Sausages with Caramelized Onion Gravy (see pages 70–71), adding extra steamed vegetables if you like.

BREAD

Slice and arrange pieces of oven-baked or grilled ready-made garlic bread on the casserole just before serving or, if you have time, make some garlic croutes by frying sliced or diced bread in olive oil and butter and then rubbing it with a cut garlic clove. Alternatively, toast some sliced ciabatta or French bread and spread it with homemade herb butter.

Buy some spiced tortilla chips and arrange them on top of chillied minced beef, chicken or lamb. Add a sprinkling of grated cheese and some torn coriander leaves. Spoon a cooked beef casserole on to warmed tortilla wraps, add a little grated cheese or soured cream, roll them up and serve with a crunchy salad. Or spoon the casserole into crisp taco shells and top in the same way.

Livening up fruit compote

Make a simple fruit compote, such as Winter Berry Compote (see page 214), and liven it up in one of the following ways.

Spoon the fruit compote into a pie dish, top with a basic crumble mix flavoured with a little grated orange rind or grated marzipan and bake in the oven until golden.

Line the base of an ovenproof dish with trifle sponges drizzled with a little sherry. Add the fruit compote, a layer of canned custard and spoonfuls of meringue. Bake in a preheated oven, 180°C (350°F), Gas Mark 4, for 15–20 minutes until the meringue is golden and the trifle is hot throughout.

Top the fruit with spoonfuls of Greek yogurt flavoured with 1–2 tablespoons lemon curd or a drizzle of honey or maple syrup.

Dip some sliced bread into 2 eggs beaten with 2 tablespoons milk, fry in a little butter until golden, then spoon the fruit on top and dust with icing sugar and a little ground cinnamon.

Spoon the compote over reheated ready-made pancakes, drop scones or toasted waffles. Top with spoonfuls of thick cream or scoops of vanilla ice cream and a drizzle of maple syrup. Spoon the cooled compote over a baked pavlova topped with whipped cream or mini meringue nests.

Caring for your slow cooker

Because a slow cooker heats food to a lower temperature than a conventional oven, cleaning is child's play: there are no burned-on splashes to deal with. To get rid of more stubborn marks, fill the slow cooker pot with warm, soapy water and leave it to soak. Use a soft cloth to wipe the inside and outside of the housing with a cream or stainless steel cleaner, depending on its finish. Never immerse the housing in water, and always make sure it is turned off before cleaning. Some, but not all, slow cooker pots are dishwasher safe, so check with your instruction manual.

Don't forget

* Some slow cookers need to be preheated before use.
* Meat, poultry, fish and dairy products must be completely defrosted before they are add to the slow cooker.
* Always add hot liquid to the pot before cooking.
* Foods will not brown in a slow cooker, so either fry ingredients first or brown the top of the finished dish by removing the slow cooker pot from the housing and browning the top under the grill.
* Don't lift the lid in the first hour of cooking while the slow cooker is heating up to a safe and optimal temperature.
* As the slow cooker heats up it forms a water seal just beneath the lid. Every time you lift the lid you break that seal and add an extra 20 minutes to the cooking time.
* The outside of the slow cooker housing gets hot when in use.
* Don't leave cooked dishes to cool down in the slow cooker when it is turned off.
* Never reheat already cooked foods in a slow cooker.

Soups

There's something comforting about a big bowl of warming soup on a cold day. They are also useful if members of your family come in at different times – everyone can just ladle out a bowlful as they need it. Soup served with a chunk of crusty bread is the ultimate TV dinner.

Vegetable broth with
mini bacon dumplings

40 g (1½ oz) butter

1 leek, sliced; white and green parts kept separate

150 g (5 oz) swede, diced

150 g (5 oz) parsnip, diced

150 g (5 oz) carrot, diced

1 celery stick, sliced

50 g (2 oz) pearl barley

1 litre (1¾ pints) boiling vegetable or chicken stock

2–3 stems of sage

1 teaspoon English mustard

salt and pepper

DUMPLINGS

75 g (3 oz) self-raising flour

40 g (1½ oz) shredded vegetable suet

2 rashers streaky bacon, finely diced

about 3 tablespoons water

Preheat the slow cooker if necessary; see the manufacturer's handbook. Heat the butter in a frying pan, add the white sliced leek and fry for 2–3 minutes until softened. Stir in the root vegetables and celery and fry for 4–5 minutes.

Add the pearl barley to the slow cooker pot. Then add the fried vegetables, the boiling stock and the sage. Stir in the mustard and a little salt and pepper. Cover with the lid and cook on low for 8–10 hours until the vegetables and barley are tender.

Make the dumplings. Put the flour, suet and bacon in a bowl with a little salt and pepper. Mix together, then gradually mix in enough water to make a soft but not sticky dough. Knead lightly on a lightly floured surface, then cut into 12 pieces. Roll into balls.

Stir the remaining green leek slices into the soup, add the dumplings, spacing them slightly apart, then replace the lid and cook on low for 45–60 minutes until light and fluffy. Ladle into bowls and serve.

Adapt this soup to use whatever winter vegetables you have, remembering to cut them into dice or cubes about 1.5 cm (¾ inch) in size so they will cook evenly in the time. If you don't have a leek you could use an onion.

PREPARATION TIME **15 minutes**

COOKING TEMPERATURE **high**

COOKING TIME **2½–3½ hours**

SERVES **4**

$\mathscr{S}$moked haddock
& bacon chowder

25 g (1 oz) butter

1 onion, finely chopped

300 g (10 oz) potatoes, cut into small dice

4 rashers smoked streaky bacon, diced

750 ml (1¼ pint) boiling fish stock

1 corn cob, leaves stripped and kernels cut away from the core, or 125 g (4 oz) frozen sweetcorn (thawed)

1 bay leaf

500 g (1 lb) smoked haddock, skinned

150 ml (¼ pint) double cream

salt and pepper

chopped parsley, to garnish

Preheat the slow cooker if necessary; see the manufacturer's handbook. Heat the butter in a frying pan, add the onion, potatoes and bacon and fry gently, stirring, until just beginning to colour.

Add to the slow cooker pot. Pour over the boiling stock, then add the sweetcorn, bay leaf and a little salt and pepper. Cover with the lid and cook on high for 2–3 hours or until the potatoes are tender.

Add the fish and press it just beneath the surface of the stock, cutting the pieces in half if needed. Replace the lid and cook for 30 minutes until the fish breaks into flakes when pressed with a knife.

Lift the fish on to a plate with a slotted spoon and break it into flakes with a knife and fork, checking for and removing any bones. Stir the cream into the soup, then return the fish. Sprinkle with parsley and serve.

This soup cooks quickly, so make sure that you chop the onion finely and cut the potatoes evenly into small dice, about 1 cm (½ inch) in size, so that they will both be cooked at the same time.

PREPARATION TIME **20 minutes**

COOKING TEMPERATURE **low**

COOKING TIME **6–8 hours**

SERVES **4**

Tomato, lentil
& aubergine soup

3–4 tablespoons olive oil, plus extra to garnish (optional)

1 aubergine, sliced

1 onion, chopped

2 garlic cloves, finely chopped

$^{1}/_{2}$ teaspoon smoked paprika (pimenton)

1 teaspoon ground cumin

125 g (4 oz) red lentils

400 g (13 oz) can chopped tomatoes

750 ml (1$^{1}/_{4}$ pint) boiling vegetable stock

salt and pepper

chopped coriander, to garnish

toasted sliced ciabatta bread, to serve (optional)

Preheat the slow cooker if necessary; see the manufacturer's handbook. Heat 1 tablespoon oil in a frying pan, add as many aubergine slices as you can to cover the base of the pan and fry them until softened and golden on both sides.

Transfer the fried aubergine to a plate, add 1–2 more tablespoons of oil and cook the rest of the aubergines. Add to the plate with the other fried aubergine slices.

Add the remaining oil to the pan and fry the onion for 5 minutes until softened. Stir in the garlic, paprika and cumin and cook for 1 minute. Mix in the lentils and tomatoes. Add a little salt and pepper, then bring to the boil. Pour the mixture into the slow cooker pot and stir in the boiling stock.

Cover with the lid and cook on low for 6–8 hours. Serve the soup as it is or purée it with a stick blender if you prefer. Ladle into bowls, drizzle with a little extra olive oil, sprinkle with coriander and serve with toasted sliced ciabatta bread.

If you have a stick blender use it to purée the soup while it is still in the slow cooker pot: it's quick, easy and saves on washing-up. Alternatively, leave the soup chunky and top it with crispy snipped streaky bacon or dry-fried pancetta slices.

PREPARATION TIME **30 minutes**

COOKING TEMPERATURE **high and low**

COOKING TIME **2¼–3¼ hours**

SERVES **4**

$\mathcal{T}$hai broth
with fish dumplings

900 ml (1½ pints) boiling fish stock

2 teaspoons Thai fish sauce
   (nam pla)

1 tablespoon red Thai curry paste

1 tablespoon soy sauce

1 bunch of spring onions, sliced

1 carrot, thinly sliced

2 garlic cloves, finely chopped

1 bunch of asparagus, trimmed and
   stems cut into 4

2 pak choi, thickly sliced, or
   200 g (7 oz) Swiss chard

DUMPLINGS

15 g (½ oz) coriander leaves

3.5 cm (1½ inches) fresh root ginger,
   peeled and sliced

400 g (13 oz) cod, skinned

1 tablespoon cornflour

1 egg white

Preheat the slow cooker if necessary; see the manufacturer's handbook. Pour the boiling fish stock into the slow cooker pot, add the fish sauce, curry paste and soy sauce. Add half the spring onions, the carrots and garlic, cover with the lid and cook on high, while making dumplings.

Put the rest of the spring onions into a food processor with the coriander and ginger and chop finely. Add the cod, cornflour and egg white and process until the fish is finely chopped.

Shape the mixture into 12 balls with wetted hands, then drop the dumplings into the slow cooker. Cover with the lid and cook on low for 2–3 hours.

Just before serving add the asparagus and pak choi to the broth. Replace the lid and cook for 15 minutes until just tender. Ladle into bowls.

If you are feeling very hungry cook 125 g (4 oz) dried egg noodles in a saucepan of boiling water, drain and place spoonfuls in the serving bowls before ladling the soup and dumplings on top.

Cheesy cauliflower soup

25 g (1 oz) butter

1 tablespoon olive oil

1 onion, chopped

1 small baking potato, about 150 g
(5 oz), cut into small dice

1 cauliflower, trimmed and cut
into florets (about 500 g (1 lb)
when prepared)

600 ml (1 pint) vegetable stock

1 teaspoon English mustard

3 teaspoons Worcestershire sauce

50 g (2 oz) Parmesan or mature
Cheddar cheese, grated

200 ml (7 fl oz) milk

a little grated nutmeg

150 ml (¼ pint) double cream

salt and pepper

croutons, to serve (optional)

Preheat the slow cooker if necessary; see the manufacturer's handbook. Heat the butter and oil in a frying pan, add the onion and potato and fry for 5 minutes or until softened but not coloured. Mix in the cauliflower, stock, mustard, Worcestershire sauce and cheese. Season with a little salt and pepper and bring to the boil.

Pour into the slow cooker pot, cover with the lid and cook on low for 4–5 hours until the vegetables are tender.

Purée the soup with a stick blender while it is still in the slow cooker or transfer it to a liquidizer and blend until smooth. Return the soup to the slow cooker pot. Stir in the milk, replace the lid and cook on high for 15 minutes until reheated. Stir and add nutmeg to taste.

Ladle into bowls, swirl cream over the top and sprinkle with a little extra nutmeg or some croutons, or both if liked.

PREPARATION TIME **25 minutes**

COOKING TEMPERATURE **low**

COOKING TIME **6¼–8¼ hours**

SERVES **4**

Carrot, orange
& fennel soup

25 g (1 oz) butter

1 tablespoon sunflower oil

1 large onion, chopped

1 teaspoon fennel seeds,
  roughly crushed

625 g (1¼ lb) carrots, diced

grated rind and juice of 1 orange

1 litre (1¾ pints) vegetable stock

salt and pepper

TO SERVE

8 tablespoons double cream

handful of croutons

Preheat the slow cooker if necessary; see the manufacturer's handbook. Heat the butter and oil in a frying pan, add the onion and fry, stirring, for 5 minutes or until the onion is just beginning to soften.

Stir in the fennel seeds and cook for 1 minute to release the flavour. Mix in the carrots, fry for 2 more minutes, then stir in the orange rind and juice. Tip into the slow cooker pot.

Bring the stock to the boil in the frying pan, add salt and pepper, then pour into the slow cooker pot. Cover with the lid and cook on low for 6–8 hours or until the carrots are tender.

Transfer to a liquidizer and purée, in batches if necessary, until smooth, then return to the slow cooker pot. Alternatively, purée the soup still in the slow cooker pot with a stick blender. Reheat if necessary in the covered slow cooker pot for 15 minutes. Ladle the soup into bowls and serve with a drizzle of cream and croutons.

PREPARATION TIME **15 minutes**

COOKING TEMPERATURE **high**

COOKING TIME **3¼ hours–4½ hours**

SERVES **4**

$\mathcal{C}$rab gumbo

1 tablespoon sunflower oil

1 onion, finely chopped

1 garlic clove, chopped

2 celery sticks, sliced

1 carrot, cut into small dice

400 g (13 oz) can chopped tomatoes

600 ml (1 pint) fish stock

50 g (2 oz) easy-cook white rice

1 bay leaf

2 stems of thyme

¼ teaspoon dried crushed red chillies

75 g (3 oz) okra, stalks trimmed and sliced

43 g (1¾ oz) can dressed crab meat

salt and pepper

TO SERVE

170 g (5¾ oz) can white crab meat (optional)

crusty bread

Preheat the slow cooker if necessary; see the manufacturer's handbook. Heat the oil in a frying pan, add the onion and fry for 5 minutes until softened. Stir in the garlic, celery and carrot, then mix in the tomatoes, stock, rice, herbs and chillies. Season with a little salt and pepper and bring to the boil.

Pour into the slow cooker pot, cover with the lid and cook on high for 3–4 hours until the vegetables and rice are tender.

Stir the soup, then add the okra and dressed crab. Replace the lid and cook for 20–30 minutes. Ladle into bowls, top with the flaked white crab meat, if liked, and serve with warm crusty bread.

If you can't get any okra add the same weight of green beans. If you like, you can also add diced red or orange peppers with the celery or a handful of prawns (thawed if frozen) along with the dressed crab at the end.

PREPARATION TIME **20 minutes**

COOKING TEMPERATURE **low**

COOKING TIME **6–8 hours**

SERVES **4**

Chunky chickpea
& chorizo soup

2 tablespoons olive oil

1 onion, chopped

2 garlic cloves, finely chopped

150 g (5 oz) chorizo, skinned
    and diced

3/4 teaspoon smoked paprika
    (pimenton)

2–3 stems of thyme

1 litre (1¾ pints) chicken stock

1 tablespoon tomato purée

375 g (12 oz) sweet potatoes, diced

410 g (13½ oz) can chickpeas,
    drained

salt and pepper

chopped parsley or extra thyme
    leaves, to garnish

Preheat the slow cooker if necessary; see the manufacturer's handbook. Heat the oil in a frying pan, add the onion and fry, stirring, for 5 minutes or until just beginning to turn golden.

Stir in the garlic and chorizo and cook for 2 minutes. Mix in the paprika, add the thyme, stock and tomato purée and bring to the boil, stirring, then add a little salt and pepper.

Add the sweet potatoes and chickpeas to the slow cooker pot and pour over the hot stock mixture. Cover with the lid and cook on low for 6–8 hours until the sweet potatoes are tender.

Ladle into bowls, sprinkle with a little chopped parsley or extra thyme and serve with warm pitta breads, if liked.

Chicken & noodle broth

1 chicken carcass

1 onion, cut into wedges

2 carrots, sliced

2 celery sticks, sliced

1 bouquet garni

1.25 litres (2¼ pints) boiling water

75 g (3 oz) vermicelli pasta

4 tablespoons chopped parsley

salt and pepper

bread, to serve (optional)

Preheat the slow cooker if necessary; see the manufacturer's handbook. Put the chicken carcass into the slow cooker pot, breaking it into 2 pieces if necessary to make it fit. Add the onion, carrots, celery and bouquet garni.

Pour over the boiling water and add a little salt and pepper. Cover with the lid and cook on high for 5–7 hours.

Strain the soup through a large sieve, then quickly pour the hot liquid back into the slow cooker pot. Take any meat off the carcass and add to the pot. Taste and adjust the seasoning if needed. Add the pasta, cover with the lid and cook on high for 20–30 minutes or until the pasta is just cooked.

Sprinkle with parsley and ladle into deep bowls. Serve with warm bread, if liked.

Light bites

Here are some smaller snacks and quick fixes for breakfast, lunch and tea. Some of the breakfasts can be put on before you go to bed so that you have a hot breakfast waiting for you when you get up in the morning.

$\mathcal{B}$reakfast compote

1 breakfast tea teabag

600 ml (1 pint) boiling water

150 g (5 oz) pitted prunes

150 g (5 oz) dried figs

75 g (3 oz) caster sugar

1 teaspoon vanilla extract

pared rind of 1/2 orange

TO SERVE

natural yogurt

muesli

Preheat the slow cooker if necessary; see the manufacturer's handbook. Put the teabag into a jug or teapot, add the boiling water and leave to infuse for 2–3 minutes. Remove the teabag and pour the tea into the slow cooker pot.

Add the whole prunes and figs, the sugar and vanilla extract to the hot tea, sprinkle with the orange rind and mix together. Cover with the lid and cook on low for 8–10 hours or overnight.

Serve hot with spoonfuls of natural yogurt and a sprinkling of muesli.

This breakfast treat also tastes delicious made with an Earl Grey tea bag to add a tang of bergamot. It can also be served warm as a dessert with cream-filled meringues or scoops of ice cream.

PREPARATION TIME **10 minutes**

COOKING TEMPERATURE **high**

COOKING TIME **40–45 minutes**

SERVES **4**

*E*ggs en cocotte
with smoked salmon

25 g (1 oz) butter

4 eggs

4 tablespoons double cream

2 teaspoons chopped chives

1 teaspoon chopped tarragon

salt and pepper

TO SERVE

200 g (7 oz) smoked salmon, sliced

4 lemon wedges

4 slices toast

Preheat the slow cooker if necessary; see the manufacturer's handbook. Liberally butter the inside of 4 x 150 ml (¼ pint) heatproof china ramekin dishes and break an egg into each one.

Drizzle the cream over the eggs and sprinkle over the herbs and a little salt and pepper. Transfer the ramekins to the slow cooker pot and pour boiling water into the pot to come halfway up the sides of the ramekins.

Cover with the lid (there is no need to cover the dishes with foil) and cook on high for 40–45 minutes or until the egg whites are set but the yolks are still slightly soft.

Lift the dishes carefully out of the slow cooker pot with a tea towel, transfer to plates and serve with smoked salmon, lemon wedges and triangles of toast.

Try ringing the changes and serve the eggs with sliced ham or grilled bacon and toasted English muffins. Alternatively you could serve them with mixed salad leaves that have been tossed in a mustard dressing.

*S*piced banana porridge

600 ml (1 pint) boiling water

300 ml (½ pint) full-fat UHT milk

150 g (5 oz) porridge oats

2 bananas

4 tablespoons light or dark
    muscovado sugar

¼ teaspoon ground cinnamon

Preheat the slow cooker if necessary; see the manufacturer's handbook. Pour the boiling water and milk into the slow cooker pot, then stir in the oats.

Cover with the lid and cook on low for 1 hour for runny porridge or 2 hours for thick porridge.

Spoon into bowls, slice the bananas and divide among the bowls. Mix together the sugar and cinnamon and sprinkle over the top. Serve immediately.

This recipe is perfect for those who like to go for a run or walk the dogs before breakfast. Put the porridge on before you go out and you will have a delicious and warming breakfast ready and waiting when you get back.

$\mathcal{B}$ig breakfast bonanza

1 tablespoon sunflower oil

12 herby chipolata sausages, about 400 g (13 oz) in total

1 onion, thinly sliced

500 g (1 lb) potatoes, peeled and cut into 2.5 cm (1 inch) chunks

375 g (12 oz) tomatoes, roughly chopped

125 g (4 oz) black pudding, peeled and cut into chunks

250 ml (8 fl oz) vegetable stock

2 tablespoons Worcestershire sauce

1 teaspoon English mustard

2–3 stems of thyme, plus extra to garnish

salt and pepper

TO SERVE

slices of white bread (optional)

4 poached eggs (optional)

Preheat the slow cooker if necessary; see the manufacturer's handbook. Heat the oil in a frying pan, add the sausages and brown on one side, turn and add the onion. Fry, turning the sausages and stirring the onions until the sausages are browned but not cooked.

Add the potatoes, tomatoes and black pudding to the slow cooker pot. Lift the sausages and onion from the pan with a slotted spoon and transfer them to the slow cooker pot. Pour off the excess fat, then add the stock, Worcestershire sauce and mustard to the pan. Tear the leaves from the thyme stems and add to pan with some salt and pepper.

Bring the sauce to the boil and pour over the sausages. Press the potatoes down so that the liquid covers them. Cover with the lid and cook on low for 9–10 hours or overnight.

Stir the dish before serving and garnish with extra thyme leaves. Serve with slices of white bread or a poached egg, if liked.

$\mathcal{E}$asy sausage & beans

1 tablespoon sunflower oil

1 onion, chopped

$^{1}/_{2}$ teaspoon smoked paprika
(pimenton)

2 x 410 g (13$^{1}/_{2}$ oz) cans baked beans

2 teaspoons wholegrain mustard

2 tablespoons Worcestershire sauce

6 tablespoons vegetable stock

2 tomatoes, roughly chopped

$^{1}/_{2}$ red pepper, cored, deseeded
and diced

350 g (11$^{1}/_{2}$ oz) chilled frankfurters,
thickly sliced

salt and pepper

buttered toast, to serve

Preheat the slow cooker if necessary; see the manufacturer's handbook.
Heat the oil in a frying pan, add the onion and fry, stirring, for
5 minutes or until softened and just beginning to turn golden.

Stir in the paprika and cook for 1 minute, then mix in the beans,
mustard, Worcestershire sauce and stock. Bring to the boil, then stir
in the tomatoes, red pepper and a little salt and pepper.

Add the frankfurters to the slow cooker pot and tip the baked bean
mixture over the top. Cover with the lid and cook on low for 9–10 hours
or overnight.

Stir well, then spoon into shallow bowls and serve with the buttered toast.

**Any leftovers can be reheated in a saucepan
or in the microwave and served with rice.
Alternatively you could try them spooned
over a crispy jacket potato served straight
from the oven.**

*C*ourgette &
broad bean frittata

40 g (1½ oz) butter

4 spring onions, sliced

1 courgette, about 200 g (7 oz),
  thinly sliced

100 g (3½ oz) podded fresh
  broad beans

6 eggs

250 ml (8 fl oz) full-fat crème
  fraîche

2 teaspoons chopped tarragon

2 tablespoons chopped parsley

salt and pepper

TO SERVE

salad

Beetroot Chutney (optional)

Preheat the slow cooker if necessary; see the manufacturer's handbook. Put the butter, onions and courgette into a bowl and cook in the microwave for 2½–3 minutes on full power until the butter has melted.

Line the slow cooker pot with a piece of nonstick baking paper, tip in the courgette and butter mix, then add the broad beans. Fork together the eggs, crème fraîche, herbs and a little salt and pepper in the bowl then pour into the slow cooker pot.

Cover with the lid and cook the frittata on high for 1½–2 hours until set in the middle. Loosen the edge with a round-bladed knife, take the slow cooker pot out of the machine with oven cloths, then cover with a large plate, invert the pot on to the plate, then remove. Peel off the lining paper and cut the frittata into wedges. Serve with salad and spoonfuls of Beetroot Chutney (see pages 218–219), if liked.

This light, summery lunch dish is ideal for anyone who is short on time, because nothing needs to be fried on the hob first. You can use frozen beans, but make sure they are thawed before you add them to the slow cooker pot.

Chillied sweetcorn

1 tablespoon sunflower oil

1 onion, finely chopped

1 orange pepper, cored, deseeded
and diced

100 g (3½ oz) frozen sweetcorn,
thawed

1 garlic clove, finely chopped

large pinch (or more to taste)
crushed dried red chillies

½ teaspoon ground cumin

1 teaspoon ground coriander

410 g (13½ oz) can mixed pulses

400 g (13 oz) can chopped tomatoes

150 ml (¼ pint) vegetable stock

2 teaspoons brown sugar

salt and pepper

TO SERVE

8 tablespoons crème fraîche

grated Cheddar cheese

4 baked potatoes (optional)

Preheat the slow cooker if necessary; see the manufacturer's handbook. Heat the oil in a frying pan, add the onion and fry for 5 minutes, stirring, until softened. Stir in the pepper, sweetcorn, garlic and spices, cook for 1 minute, then add the pulses, tomatoes, stock and sugar. Add a little salt and pepper, mix together and bring to the boil.

Pour the mixture into the slow cooker pot, cover with the lid and cook on high for 2–3 hours.

Serve the chilli with crème fraîche and cheese, or spooned on top of jacket potatoes.

You could add 250 g (8 oz) extra lean minced beef when you are frying the onion. Increase the cooking time to 3–4 hours. An alternative to serving with jacket potatoes is to top the chilli with tortilla chips, crème fraîche and grated cheese.

$\mathcal{M}$editerranean
roasted vegetable terrine

375 g (12 oz) courgettes, thinly
sliced

1 red pepper, quartered, deseeded
and cored

1 orange pepper, quartered, deseeded
and cored

2 tablespoons olive oil

1 garlic clove, finely chopped

2 eggs

150 ml (¼ pint) full-fat milk

25 g (1 oz) Parmesan cheese, grated

3 tablespoons chopped basil

salt and pepper

salad, to serve (optional)

Preheat the slow cooker if necessary; see the manufacturer's handbook.
Line the grill rack with foil. Arrange all the vegetables on the foil in
a single layer, with the peppers skin side up. Drizzle with the oil and
sprinkle with the garlic and salt and pepper.

Grill the vegetables for 10 minutes or until softened and browned.
Transfer the courgette slices to a plate and wrap the peppers in the foil.
Leave to stand for 5 minutes to loosen the skins.

In a bowl beat together the eggs, milk, Parmesan, basil and a little
salt and pepper. Lightly oil a 500 g (1 lb) loaf tin and line the base and
2 long sides with a piece of nonstick baking paper.

Unwrap the peppers, peel away the skins with a small, sharp knife and
add any juices in the foil to the custard. Arrange one-third of the
courgette slices over the base of the tin or until covered. Spoon in a little
of the basil custard, then add the red peppers and a little more custard.
Repeat, ending with a layer of courgettes and custard. Cover the top
loosely with oiled foil and put in the slow cooker pot.

Pour boiling water into the slow cooker to come halfway up the sides
of the tin. Cover with the lid and cook on high for 2–3 hours or until
the custard is set. Take the tin out of the slow cooker with a tea towel
and leave to cool.

Loosen the edge of the terrine with a round-bladed knife. Invert the tin
on to a chopping board and peel away the paper. Cut the terrine into
slices and serve with salad, if liked.

$\mathcal{D}$uck, pork &
apple rillettes

2 duck legs

500 g (1 lb) rashers rindless pork belly, halved

1 onion, cut into wedges

1 sharp dessert apple, such as Granny Smith, peeled, cored and thickly sliced

2–3 sprigs of thyme

250 ml (8 fl oz) chicken stock

150 ml (¼ pint) dry cider

salt and pepper

TO SERVE

crusty bread

radishes

pickled shallots (optional)

Preheat the slow cooker if necessary; see the manufacturer's handbook. Put the duck and belly pork into the base of the slow cooker pot. Tuck the onion and apple between the pieces of meat and add the thyme.

Pour the stock and cider into a saucepan, add plenty of salt and pepper and bring to the boil.

Pour the hot liquid into the slow cooker pot, cover with the lid and cook on high for 5–6 hours until the duck and pork are tender.

Leave to cool for 30 minutes, then lift the meat out of the slow cooker pot with a slotted spoon and transfer it to a large plate. Peel away the duck skin and remove the bones. Shred the meat into small pieces with a knife and fork. Discard the thyme sprigs. Scoop out the apple and onion with a slotted spoon and finely chop. Mix the apple and onion with the meat, then taste and adjust the seasoning if necessary.

Pack the chopped meat mix into 4 individual dishes or small 'le parfait' jars and press down firmly. Spoon over the juices still remaining in the slow cooker pot to cover and seal the meat, then leave to cool. Transfer to the refrigerator and chill well. When the fat has solidified on the top, cover each dish with a lid or clingfilm. They can be kept in the refrigerator for up to 1 week.

Serve the rillettes with warm crusty bread, a few radishes and pickled shallots, if liked.

PREPARATION TIME **30 minutes**

COOKING TEMPERATURE **high**

COOKING TIME **5–6 hours**

SERVES **4–6**

*T*urkey, cranberry
& orange meatloaf

115 g (3¾ oz) pack dried orange and cranberry stuffing mix

25 g (1 oz) dried cranberries

1 tablespoon sunflower oil

1 onion, finely chopped

500 g (1 lb) skinless turkey breast steaks

200 g (7 oz) smoked streaky bacon

1 egg, beaten

salt and pepper

TO SERVE

salad

cranberry sauce (optional)

Beetroot Chutney (optional)

Put the stuffing mix in a bowl, add the cranberries and mix with boiling water as the instructions on the stuffing pack direct.

Heat the oil in a frying pan, add the onion and fry for 5 minutes, stirring, until softened. Set aside. Finely chop the turkey slices in a food processor or pass through a coarse mincer.

Meanwhile, preheat the slow cooker if necessary; see the manufacturer's handbook. Take a soufflé dish that is 14 cm (5½ inches) in diameter and 9 cm (3½ inches) high and line the base with greaseproof or nonstick baking paper. Stretch each rasher of bacon with the flat of a large cook's knife until half as long again, and use about three-quarters of the rashers to line the base and sides of the dish, trimming to fit as necessary.

Mix the stuffing with the fried onion, chopped turkey and egg. Season well and spoon into the bacon-lined dish. Press flat and cover with the remaining rashers of bacon.

Cover the dish with foil and lower into the slow cooker pot. Pour boiling water into the pot to come halfway up the sides of the dish, then add the lid and cook on high for 5–6 hours or until the juices run clear when the centre of the meatloaf is pierced with a small knife.

Lift the dish out of the slow cooker with oven gloves. Leave the meatloaf to cool in the dish, then chill in the refrigerator overnight until firm. Loosen the edge with a round-bladed knife, turn out and peel off the lining paper. Cut into thick slices and serve with salad and spoonfuls of cranberry sauce or Beetroot Chutney (see pages 218–219), if liked.

PREPARATION TIME **20 minutes**

COOKING TEMPERATURE **low**

COOKING TIME **9–10 hours**

or overnight

SERVES **4**

$\mathcal{P}$otato, apple & bacon hotpot

750 g (1½ lb) potatoes, thinly sliced

25 g (1 oz) butter

1 tablespoon sunflower oil

2 onions, roughly chopped

250 g (8 oz) smoked back bacon, diced

1 dessert apple, cored and sliced

2 tablespoons plain flour

450 ml (¾ pint) chicken stock

2 teaspoons English mustard

2 bay leaves

50 g (2 oz) Cheddar cheese, grated

salt and pepper

grilled tomato halves, to serve (optional)

Preheat the slow cooker if necessary; see the manufacturer's handbook. Bring a large saucepan of water to the boil, add the potatoes, cook for 3 minutes, then drain.

Heat the butter and oil in a frying pan, add the onions and bacon and fry, stirring, for 5 minutes or until just beginning to turn golden. Stir in the apple and flour and season the mixture well with salt and pepper.

Layer the potatoes and the onion mixture in the slow cooker pot, ending with a layer of potatoes. Add the stock and mustard to the frying pan, bring to the boil, then pour into the slow cooker pot. And add the bay leaves. Cover with the lid and cook on low for 9–10 hours.

Sprinkle the top of the potatoes with the cheese, lift the pot out of the housing using oven gloves and brown under a preheated hot grill. Spoon into shallow bowls and serve with grilled tomato halves, if liked.

PREPARATION TIME **15 minutes**

COOKING TEMPERATURE **high**

COOKING TIME **40–60 minutes**

SERVES **4**

$\mathcal{B}$eery cheese fondue

15 g (¹/₂ oz) butter

2 shallots or ¹/₂ small onion,
    finely chopped

1 garlic clove, finely chopped

3 teaspoons cornflour

200 ml (7 fl oz) blond beer or lager

200 g (7 oz) Gruyère cheese (rind
    removed), grated

175 g (6 oz) Emmental cheese (rind
    removed), grated

grated nutmeg

salt and pepper

TO SERVE

¹/₂ wholewheat French stick, cubed

2 celery sticks, cut into short lengths

8 small pickled onions, drained
    and halved

1 bunch of radishes, tops trimmed

1 red pepper, cored, deseeded
    and cubed

2 endive, leaves separated

Preheat the slow cooker if necessary; see the manufacturer's handbook. Butter the inside of the slow cooker pot, then add the shallots or onion and garlic.

Put the cornflour in a small bowl, add a little of the beer and mix to make a smooth paste. Blend in the remaining beer. Add to the slow cooker with both cheeses, a little nutmeg and some salt and pepper.

Stir together, cover with the lid and cook on high for 40–60 minutes, whisking once during cooking. Whisk again and serve with the dippers arranged on a serving plate, with long fondue or ordinary forks for dunking the dippers into the fondue.

Everyday suppers

Do you sometimes feel that you add the same ingredients to your supermarket trolley every week as if you are on automatic pilot? Ring the changes with some tasty twists to old favourites and encourage the children to try something new too.

*C*idered pork
with sage dumplings

1 tablespoon sunflower oil

750 g (1½ lb) pork shoulder steaks, cubed and any fat discarded

1 leek, thinly sliced; white and green parts kept separate

2 tablespoons plain flour

300 ml (½ pint) dry cider

300 ml (½ pint) chicken stock

200 g (7 oz) carrot, diced

1 dessert apple, cored and diced

2–3 stems of sage

salt and pepper

DUMPLINGS

150 g (5 oz) self-raising flour

75 g (3 oz) vegetable suet

1 tablespoon chopped sage

2 tablespoons chopped parsley

5–7 tablespoons water

Preheat the slow cooker if necessary; see the manufacturer's handbook. Heat the oil in a frying pan, add the pork a few pieces at a time until all the pieces are in the pan, then fry over a high heat until lightly browned. Lift the pork out of the pan with a slotted spoon and transfer it to the slow cooker pot.

Add the white leek slices to the pan and fry for 2–3 minutes or until softened. Stir in the flour, then gradually mix in the cider and stock. Add the carrot, apple, sage and some salt and pepper. Bring to the boil, stirring continuously.

Pour the mixture into the slow cooker pot, cover with the lid and cook on low for 8–10 hours or until the pork is tender.

Make the dumplings. Put the flour, suet, herbs and a little salt and pepper into a bowl, mix together, then gradually stir in enough water to make a soft but not sticky dough. Cut into 12 pieces and roll them into balls with floured hands.

Stir the green leek slices into the casserole and arrange the dumplings on the top. Cover with the lid and cook, still on low, for 1 hour until they are well risen. Spoon the stew into shallow bowls to serve.

$\mathscr{M}$ustard chicken &
bacon casserole

15 g (½ oz) butter

1 tablespoon sunflower oil

4 chicken thighs and 4 chicken
   drumstick joints

4 rashers smoked back bacon, diced

400 g (13 oz) leeks, thinly sliced;
   white and green parts kept
   separate

2 tablespoons plain flour

600 ml (1 pint) chicken stock

3 teaspoons wholegrain mustard

salt and pepper

mashed potatoes, to serve (optional)

Preheat the slow cooker if necessary; see the manufacturer's handbook. Heat the butter and oil in a frying pan, add the chicken joints and fry over a high heat until browned on all sides. Remove from the pan with a slotted spoon and transfer to the slow cooker pot.

Add the bacon and white leek slices to the frying pan and fry, stirring, for 5 minutes or until just beginning to turn golden. Stir in the flour, then gradually mix in the stock, mustard and a little salt and pepper. Bring to the boil. Pour into the slow cooker pot, cover with the lid and cook on low for 8–10 hours.

Add the green leek slices and stir into the sauce. Replace the lid and cook, still on low, for 15 minutes or until the green leeks are just softened. Spoon the casserole into shallow serving bowls and serve with mashed potatoes, if liked.

For a different take on this dish, replace a quarter of the chicken stock with 150 ml (¼ pint) red wine or cider, omit the leeks and mustard and add shallots and a bouquet garni. Or you could try adding a few stoned prunes or dried chestnuts to the casserole.

PREPARATION TIME **30 minutes**

COOKING TEMPERATURE **low**

COOKING TIME **8¾–11¼ hours**

SERVES **4**

$\mathscr{M}$oussaka

4 tablespoons olive oil

1 large aubergine, thinly sliced

500 g (1 lb) minced lamb

1 onion, chopped

2 garlic cloves, finely chopped

1 tablespoon plain flour

400 g (13 oz) can chopped tomatoes

200 ml (7 fl oz) lamb stock

1 teaspoon ground cinnamon

¼ teaspoon grated nutmeg

1 tablespoon tomato purée

salt and pepper

salad, to serve (optional)

TOPPING

3 eggs

250 g (8 oz) natural yogurt

75 g (3 oz) feta cheese, grated

pinch of grated nutmeg

Preheat the slow cooker if necessary; see the manufacturer's handbook. Heat half the oil in a frying pan and fry the aubergine slices in batches, adding more oil as needed until they have all been fried and are softened and lightly browned on both sides. Drain and transfer to a plate.

Add the minced lamb and onion to the frying pan and dry-fry, stirring and breaking up the lamb, until evenly browned. Stir in the garlic and flour, then mix in the tomatoes, stock, spices, tomato purée and a little salt and pepper. Bring to the boil, stirring.

Spoon the lamb mixture into the slow cooker pot and arrange the aubergine slices on top, overlapping them to cover the top evenly. Cover with the lid and cook on low for 8–10 hours.

Make the custard topping. Mix together the eggs, yogurt, feta and nutmeg. Spoon the mixture over the aubergines, replace the lid and cook, still on low, for ¾–1¼ hours or until set. Lift the pot out of the housing using oven gloves and brown under a hot grill. Serve with salad.

Although not very Greek, this dish can be served without the custard topping, adding mashed potatoes flavoured with yogurt or Cheddar cheese instead. You could also simply spoon the meaty mixture on top of a dish of rice.

$\mathscr{M}$ackerel with
harissa potatoes

500 g (1 lb) new potatoes, scrubbed and thickly sliced

1 tablespoon olive oil

1 onion, chopped

$^{1}/_{2}$ red pepper, cored, deseeded and diced

$^{1}/_{2}$ yellow pepper, cored, deseeded and diced

1 garlic clove, finely chopped

2 teaspoons harissa (Moroccan chilli paste)

200 g (7 oz) tomatoes, roughly chopped

1 tablespoon tomato purée

300 ml ($^{1}/_{2}$ pint) fish stock

4 small mackerel, each about 300 g (10 oz), gutted and heads removed

salt and pepper

pitta breads, to serve (optional)

Preheat the slow cooker if necessary; see the manufacturer's handbook. Bring a saucepan of water to the boil, add the potatoes and cook for 4–5 minutes or until almost tender. Drain and reserve.

Heat the oil in a frying pan, add the onion and fry, stirring, for 5 minutes or until softened and just beginning to turn golden. Stir in the peppers and garlic and fry for 2–3 minutes. Mix in the harissa, tomatoes, tomato purée, stock and a little salt and pepper and bring to the boil.

Tip the potatoes into the slow cooker pot. Rinse the fish well, drain and arrange in a single layer on top of the potatoes, then cover with the hot tomato mixture. Cover with the lid and cook on low for 5–7 hours or until the potatoes are tender and the fish flakes when pressed in the centre with a small knife.

Spoon into shallow bowls and serve with warmed pitta breads, if liked.

Mackerel are surprisingly cheap and are a rich source of omega 3 fatty acids, which are thought to boost brain power and help protect against heart and circulation problems.

PREPARATION TIME **20 minutes**

COOKING TEMPERATURE **low**

COOKING TIME **6–8 hours**

SERVES **4**

𝒮ausages with
caramelized onion gravy

1 tablespoon sunflower oil

8 speciality flavoured sausages, such
    as Sicilian or Toulouse

2 red onions, halved and thinly sliced

2 teaspoons light muscovado sugar

2 tablespoons plain flour

450 ml (¾ pint) beef stock

1 tablespoon sun-dried or ordinary
    tomato purée

1 bay leaf

salt and pepper

TO SERVE

carrots

broccoli

Preheat the slow cooker if necessary; see the manufacturer's handbook. Heat the oil in a frying pan, add the sausages and fry over a high heat for 5 minutes, turning until browned on all sides but not cooked through. Drain and transfer to the slow cooker pot.

Add the onions to the frying pan and fry over a medium heat for 5 minutes or until softened. Add the sugar and fry, stirring, for 5 more minutes or until the onion slices are caramelized around the edges.

Stir in the flour, then gradually mix in the stock. Add the tomato purée, the bay leaf and some salt and pepper and bring to the boil, still stirring. Pour over the sausages. Cover with the lid and cook on low for 6–8 hours or until the sausages are cooked through.

Serve the sausages and gravy spooned into reheated ready-made large Yorkshire puddings and accompanied with steamed carrots and broccoli.

If you are opening a bottle of beer to drink with the meal, you could reduce the amount of stock to 400 ml (14 fl oz) and add a splash of beer at the very end of cooking.

PREPARATION TIME **25 minutes**

COOKING TEMPERATURE **high**

COOKING TIME **5–7 hours**

SERVES **4**

Maple-glazed ribs

1.25 kg (2½ lb) pork ribs, rinsed with cold water and drained

1 onion, quartered

1 carrot, thickly sliced

2 bay leaves

2 tablespoons malt vinegar

1 teaspoon black peppercorns

½ teaspoon salt

1 litre (1¾ pints) boiling water

GLAZE

2 teaspoons English mustard

1 teaspoon ground allspice

2 tablespoons tomato purée

2 tablespoons brown sugar

125 ml (4 fl oz) maple syrup

COLESLAW

2 carrots, grated

¼ red cabbage, shredded

3 spring onions, sliced

100 g (3½ oz) sweetcorn (thawed if frozen)

2 tablespoons mayonnaise

2 tablespoons natural yogurt

Preheat the slow cooker if necessary; see the manufacturer's handbook. Put the pork, onion, carrot, bay leaves, vinegar, peppercorns, salt and boiling water into the slow cooker pot, cover with the lid and cook on high for 5–7 hours or until the ribs are tender.

Remove the ribs from the slow cooker with a slotted spoon and transfer to a foil-lined grill pan. Mix together the ingredients for the glaze with 150 ml (¼ pint) hot stock from the slow cooker pot. Spoon the glaze over the ribs, then grill for 10–15 minutes, turning once or twice, until browned and sticky.

Meanwhile, mix together the ingredients for the coleslaw and spoon into 4 small bowls. Place these on dinner plates, then pile the ribs on to the plates to serve.

In the summertime you can barbecue the glazed ribs (minus the stock) over preheated coals, dousing any flames from the juices spitting on the coals with a water sprayer. This will give the sweet and sticky ribs a wonderful smoky flavour.

PREPARATION TIME **20 minutes**

COOKING TEMPERATURE **low**

COOKING TIME **8–10 hours**

SERVES **4**

Gourmet bolognese

1 tablespoon olive oil

500 g (1 lb) lean minced beef

1 onion, chopped

225 g (7½ oz) chicken livers
    (thawed if frozen)

2 garlic cloves, finely chopped

50 g (2 oz) pancetta or smoked back
    bacon, diced

150 g (5 oz) cup mushrooms, sliced

1 tablespoon plain flour

150 ml (¼ pint) red wine

150 ml (¼ pint) beef stock

400 g (13 oz) can chopped tomatoes

2 tablespoons tomato purée

1 bouquet garni

salt and pepper

300 g (10 oz) tagliatelle

TO SERVE

shaved Parmesan cheese

basil leaves

Preheat the slow cooker if necessary; see the manufacturer's handbook. Heat the oil in a frying pan, add the mince and onion and fry, stirring and breaking up the mince with a spoon until it is evenly browned.

Meanwhile, rinse the chicken livers in a sieve, drain and chop roughly, discarding any white cores. Add to the frying pan with the garlic, pancetta or bacon and mushrooms and cook for 2–3 minutes or until the livers are browned.

Stir in the flour, then mix in the wine, stock, tomatoes, tomato purée, bouquet garni and salt and pepper. Bring to the boil, stirring. Spoon into the slow cooker pot, cover with the lid and cook on low for 8–10 hours.

Just before serving put the tagliatelle into a saucepan of boiling salted water and cook for 8 minutes or until just tender. Drain and stir into the bolognese. Spoon into shallow bowls and sprinkle with Parmesan shavings and some basil leaves.

Bolognese sauce does not have to be made with minced beef despite what the traditionalists say; try minced lamb or even minced pork for a change. You could also shape the beef and livers into meatballs if preferred.

Cheesy macaroni
with smoked haddock

200 g (7 oz) macaroni

1 tablespoon olive oil

1 onion, chopped

50 g (2 oz) butter

50 g (2 oz) plain flour

450 ml (¾ pint) full-fat UHT milk

450 ml (¾ pint) fish stock

175 g (6 oz) Cheddar cheese, grated

¼ teaspoon grated nutmeg

500 g (1 lb) smoked haddock,
skinned and cut into 2.5 cm
(1 inch) cubes

200 g (7 oz) can sweetcorn, drained

125 g (4 oz) spinach, rinsed, drained
and roughly torn

salt and pepper

cherry tomatoes, to serve

Preheat the slow cooker if necessary; see the manufacturer's handbook. Tip the macaroni into a bowl, cover with plenty of boiling water and leave to stand for 10 minutes while you prepare the rest of the dish.

Heat the oil in a saucepan, add the onion and fry gently, stirring, for 5 minutes or until softened. Add the butter and, when melted, stir in the flour. Gradually mix in the milk and bring to the boil, stirring until smooth. Stir in the stock, 125 g (4 oz) of the Cheddar, nutmeg and salt and pepper and bring back to the boil, stirring.

Drain the macaroni and add to the slow cooker pot with the haddock and sweetcorn. Pour over the sauce and gently stir together. Cover with the lid and cook on low for 2–3 hours.

Stir the spinach into the macaroni, replace the lid and cook, still on low, for 15 minutes. Lift the pot out of the housing using oven gloves and stir once more. Sprinkle the remaining Cheddar over the macaroni, then brown under a preheated hot grill until the top is golden. Serve with grilled cherry tomatoes on the vine.

PREPARATION TIME **25 minutes**

COOKING TEMPERATURE **high**

COOKING TIME **7–8 hours**

SERVES **4**

Beef hotpot

1 tablespoon sunflower oil

750 g (1½ lb) braising beef, cubed

1 onion, chopped

2 tablespoons plain flour

600 ml (1 pint) beef stock

2 tablespoons Worcestershire sauce

1 tablespoon tomato purée

2 teaspoons English mustard

3 sprigs of rosemary

125 g (4 oz) carrots, diced

125 g (4 oz) swede, diced

125 g (4 oz) parsnip, diced

700 g (1 lb 6 oz) potatoes,
  thinly sliced

25 g (1 oz) butter

salt and pepper

Preheat the slow cooker if necessary; see the manufacturer's handbook. Heat the oil in a frying pan, add the beef a few pieces at a time until all the meat is in the pan, then fry over a high heat, stirring, until browned. Remove the beef from the pan with a slotted spoon and transfer to the slow cooker pot.

Add the onion to the pan and fry, stirring, for 5 minutes or until softened and just beginning to turn golden. Stir in the flour, then gradually mix in the stock. Add the Worcestershire sauce, tomato purée, mustard and leaves from 2 sprigs of the rosemary. Season with salt and pepper and bring to the boil, stirring.

Add the diced vegetables to the slow cooker pot. Pour the onion and sauce over them, then cover with the potato slices, arranging them so that they overlap and pressing them down into the stock. Sprinkle with the leaves torn from the remaining stem of rosemary and a little salt and pepper.

Cover with the lid and cook on high for 7–8 hours until the potatoes are tender. Lift the pot out of the housing using oven gloves; dot the potatoes with the butter and brown under a preheated hot grill, if liked.

Chicken korma

2 tablespoons sunflower oil

8 chicken thighs, about 1 kg (2 lb) in total, skinned, boned and cubed

2 onions, finely chopped, plus extra to garnish

1–2 green chillies (or to taste), deseeded and finely chopped

2.5 cm (1 inch) fresh root ginger, peeled and finely chopped

5 tablespoons korma curry paste

250 ml (8 fl oz) coconut cream or coconut milk

300 ml (½ pint) chicken stock

2 tablespoons ground almonds

small bunch of coriander

200 g (7 oz) natural yogurt

2 tomatoes, diced

salt and pepper

chapattis, to serve

Preheat the slow cooker if necessary; see the manufacturer's handbook. Heat the oil in a frying pan, add the chicken a few pieces at a time until they are all in the pan, then fry, stirring, until golden. Remove the chicken from the pan with a slotted spoon and put it in the slow cooker pot.

Add the onions, chillies, ginger and curry paste to the pan and fry, stirring, for 2–3 minutes. Pour in the coconut cream or milk, stock and ground almonds. Tear half the coriander into pieces and add to the sauce with a little salt and pepper. Bring to the boil, stirring, then spoon over the chicken.

Cover with the lid and cook on low for 6–8 hours.

Stir the korma, then ladle it into bowls, top with spoonfuls of yogurt, the tomatoes and extra raw onion and the remaining coriander torn into small pieces. Serve with warm chapattis.

Rather than buying a take-away, make the curry, cool, then pack into individual plastic boxes. Freeze and then transfer to the refrigerator the night before you need it or first thing in the morning to defrost. Reheat in the microwave when you get home.

$\mathscr{R}$ancheros pie

1 tablespoon sunflower oil

500 g (1 lb) minced beef

1 onion, chopped

2 garlic cloves, finely chopped

1 teaspoon cumin seeds, roughly crushed

^{1}/$_4$–^{1}/$_2$ teaspoon crushed dried red chillies

^{1}/$_4$ teaspoon ground allspice

2 stems of oregano, roughly chopped

3 tablespoons sultanas

400 g (13 oz) can chopped tomatoes

250 ml (8 fl oz) beef stock

salt and pepper

TOPPING

500 g (1 lb) sweet potatoes, thinly sliced

25 g (1 oz) butter

a few crushed dried red chillies

Preheat the slow cooker if necessary; see the manufacturer's handbook. Heat the oil in a frying pan, add the beef and onion and fry, stirring and breaking up the mince with a wooden spoon, until browned.

Stir in the garlic, spices, oregano, sultanas, tomatoes and stock. Add a little salt and pepper and bring to the boil, stirring. Spoon into the slow cooker pot, cover with overlapping slices of sweet potato, dot with butter and sprinkle with dried chillies and a little salt and pepper.

Cover with the lid and cook on low for 7–8 hours until the potato topping is tender. Lift the pot out of the housing using oven gloves and brown under a preheated hot grill, if liked.

PREPARATION TIME **20 minutes**

COOKING TEMPERATURE **low**

COOKING TIME **4–5 hours**

SERVES **4**

$\mathscr{T}$una arrabiata

1 tablespoon olive oil

1 onion, chopped

2 garlic cloves, finely chopped

1 red pepper, cored, deseeded and diced

1 teaspoon smoked paprika (pimenton)

1/4–1/2 teaspoon crushed dried red chillies

400 g (13 oz) can chopped tomatoes

150 ml (1/4 pint) vegetable or fish stock

200 g (7 oz) can tuna in water, drained

375 g (12 oz) spaghetti

salt and pepper

TO SERVE

freshly grated Parmesan cheese

basil leaves

Preheat the slow cooker if necessary; see the manufacturer's handbook. Heat the oil in a frying pan, add the onion and fry, stirring, for 5 minutes or until just beginning to turn golden around the edges.

Stir in the garlic, red pepper, paprika and dried chillies and cook for 2 minutes. Mix in the tomatoes, stock and a little salt and pepper. Bring to the boil, then tip into the slow cooker pot. Break the tuna into large pieces and stir into the tomato mixture. Cover with the lid and cook on low for 4–5 hours.

When almost ready to serve, bring a large saucepan of water to the boil, add the spaghetti and cook for about 8 minutes or until tender. Drain and stir into the tomato sauce. Spoon into shallow bowls and serve sprinkled with grated Parmesan and basil leaves.

PREPARATION TIME **15 minutes**

COOKING TEMPERATURE **low**

COOKING TIME **8–10 hours**

SERVES **4**

$\mathcal{L}$amb tagine
with figs & almonds

1 tablespoon olive oil

750 g (1½ lb) lamb fillet, diced,
    or ready-diced lamb

1 onion, sliced

2 garlic cloves, finely chopped

2.5 cm (1 inch) fresh root ginger,
    peeled and finely chopped

2 tablespoons plain flour

600 ml (1 pint) lamb stock

1 teaspoon ground cinnamon

2 large pinches of saffron threads

75 g (3 oz) dried figs, stalks
    trimmed off and fruits diced

40 g (1½ oz) toasted flaked almonds

salt and pepper

lemon and chickpea couscous,
    to serve

Preheat the slow cooker if necessary; see the manufacturer's handbook. Heat the oil in a frying pan, add the lamb a few pieces at a time until all the pieces are added to the pan, then fry over a high heat, stirring until browned. Remove from the pan with a slotted spoon and transfer to the slow cooker pot.

Add the onion to the frying pan and fry, stirring, for 5 minutes or until softened and just beginning to turn golden. Stir in the garlic and ginger, then mix in the flour. Gradually stir in the stock. Add the spices, figs and a little salt and pepper and bring to the boil, stirring.

Spoon into the slow cooker pot, cover with the lid and cook on low for 8–10 hours or until the lamb is tender. Stir, then sprinkle with toasted flaked almonds. Serve with lemon and chickpea couscous.

To make couscous, put 200 g (7 oz) couscous in a bowl with the grated rind and juice of 1 lemon, 2 tablespoons olive oil, 410 g (13½ oz) can drained chick peas, 450 ml (¾ pint) boiling water and season. Stand for 5 minutes then fork in 4 tablespoons chopped coriander.

$\mathcal{B}$eery barley beef

1 tablespoon sunflower oil

625 g (1¼ lb) lean stewing beef,
    cubed

1 onion, chopped

1 tablespoon plain flour

250 g (8 oz) carrots, diced

250 g (8 oz) parsnips or potatoes,
    diced

300 ml (½ pint) light ale

750 ml (1¼ pints) beef stock

small bunch of mixed herbs or dried
    bouquet garni

100 g (3½ oz) pearl barley

salt and pepper

Preheat the slow cooker if necessary; see the manufacturer's handbook.
Heat the oil in a frying pan, add the beef a few pieces at a time until
it is all in the pan, then fry over a high heat, stirring, until browned.
Remove the beef with a slotted spoon and transfer to the slow cooker pot.

Add the onion to the frying pan and fry, stirring, for 5 minutes or until
lightly browned. Mix in the flour, then add the diced vegetables and
beer and bring to the boil, stirring. Pour into the slow cooker pot.

Add the stock to the frying pan with the herbs and a little salt and
pepper, bring to the boil, then pour into the slow cooker pot. Stir in the
pearl barley, cover with the lid and cook on low for 9–10 hours until
the beef is tender.

**Pearl barley swells as it cooks so you may
find that you need to add a little extra stock
at the end of the cooking time or when you
are reheating any leftovers to avoid the dish
drying out.**

PREPARATION TIME **20 minutes**

COOKING TEMPERATURE **low**

COOKING TIME **6¼–8¼ hours**

SERVES **4**

$\mathscr{S}$weet & sour chicken

1 tablespoon sunflower oil

8 small chicken thighs, about 1 kg (2 lb) in total, skinned, boned and cubed

4 spring onions, thickly sliced; white and green parts kept separate

2 carrots, halved lengthways and thinly sliced

2.5 cm (1 inch) fresh root ginger, peeled and finely chopped

430 g (14¼ oz) can pineapple chunks in natural juice

300 ml (½ pint) chicken stock

1 tablespoon cornflour

1 tablespoon tomato purée

2 tablespoons caster sugar

2 tablespoons soy sauce

2 tablespoons malt vinegar

225 g (7½ oz) can bamboo shoots, drained

125 g (4 oz) bean sprouts

100 g (3½ oz) mangetout, thinly sliced

rice, to serve

Preheat the slow cooker if necessary; see the manufacturer's handbook. Heat the oil in a frying pan, add the chicken thighs and fry, stirring, until browned on all sides. Mix in the white spring onion slices, carrots and ginger and cook for 2 minutes.

Stir in the pineapple chunks with their juice and the stock. Put the cornflour, tomato purée and sugar into a small bowl, then gradually mix in the soy sauce and vinegar to make a smooth paste. Stir into the frying pan and bring to the boil, stirring.

Tip the chicken and sauce into the slow cooker pot, add the bamboo shoots and press the chicken beneath the surface of the sauce. Cover with the lid and cook on low for 6–8 hours.

When almost ready to serve, add the green spring onion slices, the bean sprouts and mangetout to the slow cooker pot and mix well. Replace the lid and cook, still on low, for 15 minutes or until the vegetables are just tender. Serve spooned into rice-filled bowls.

PREPARATION TIME **20 minutes**

COOKING TEMPERATURE **low**

COOKING TIME **8–10 hours**

SERVES **4**

Chillied beef
with cheesy tortillas

1 tablespoon sunflower oil

500 g (1 lb) extra lean minced beef

1 onion, chopped

2 garlic cloves, finely chopped

1 teaspoon smoked paprika
(pimenton)

1/2 teaspoon crushed dried red chillies

1 teaspoon ground cumin

1 tablespoon plain flour

400 g (13 oz) can chopped tomatoes

410 g (13 1/2 oz) can red kidney
beans, drained

150 ml (1/4 pint) beef stock

1 tablespoon dark muscovado sugar

salt and pepper

TOPPING

100 g (3 1/2 oz) tortilla chips

1/2 red pepper, cored, deseeded and
diced

chopped coriander leaves

100 g (3 1/2 oz) mature Cheddar
cheese, grated

Preheat the slow cooker if necessary; see the manufacturer's handbook. Heat the oil in a frying pan, add the mince and onion and fry, stirring, for 5 minutes, breaking up the mince with a spoon until it is browned.

Stir in the garlic, paprika, chillies and cumin and cook for 2 minutes. Stir in the flour. Mix in the tomatoes, kidney beans, stock and sugar, season with salt and pepper and pour the mixture into the slow cooker pot. Cover with the lid and cook on low for 8–10 hours.

Stir the mixture, then arrange the tortilla chips on top. Sprinkle over the red pepper, coriander and Cheddar, lift the pot out of the housing using oven gloves and brown under a preheated hot grill until the cheese just melts. Spoon into bowls to serve.

If you have any beef left over from this dish, serve it spooned over jacket potatoes or sweet jacket potatoes then top with soured cream and grated Cheddar cheese and sprinkle with a handful of torn coriander leaves.

PREPARATION TIME **15 minutes**

COOKING TEMPERATURE **low**

COOKING TIME **3¹/₄–4¹/₄ hours**

SERVES **4**

$\mathcal{M}$ackerel kedgeree

1 tablespoon sunflower oil

1 onion, chopped

1 teaspoon turmeric

2 tablespoons mango chutney

750–900 ml (1¹/₄–1¹/₂ pints)
    vegetable stock

1 bay leaf

175 g (6 oz) easy-cook brown rice

250 g (8 oz) or 3 smoked mackerel
    fillets, skinned

100 g (3¹/₂ oz) frozen peas

25 g (1 oz) watercress or
    rocket leaves

salt and pepper

4 hard-boiled eggs, cut into wedges,
    to garnish

Preheat the slow cooker if necessary; see the manufacturer's handbook. Heat the oil in a frying pan, add the onion and fry, stirring, for 5 minutes or until softened and just beginning to turn golden.

Stir in the turmeric, chutney, stock, bay leaf and a little salt and pepper and bring to the boil. Pour into the slow cooker pot and add the rice. Add the smoked mackerel to the pot in a single layer. Cover with the lid and cook on low for 3–4 hours or until the rice is tender and has absorbed almost all the stock.

Stir in the peas, breaking up the fish into chunky pieces. Add extra hot stock if needed. Cook for 15 minutes more. Stir in the watercress or rocket, spoon on to plates and serve garnished with wedges of egg.

$\mathcal{S}$piced meatballs
with dill sauce

1 onion, quartered

50 g (2 oz) bread

250 g (8 oz) minced pork

250 g (8 oz) minced beef

1 teaspoon ground mixed spice

1 egg yolk

1 tablespoon sunflower oil

salt and pepper

SAUCE

15 g (½ oz) butter

1 onion, sliced

2 tablespoons plain flour

600 ml (1 pint) chicken stock

4 teaspoons chopped dill, plus
    extra to garnish

Preheat the slow cooker if necessary; see the manufacturer's handbook. Finely chop the onion and bread in a food processor or blender. Add the minced meats, mixed spice, egg yolk and a little salt and pepper and mix together.

Divide the meat mixture into 24 pieces and roll into balls with wetted hands. Heat the oil in a frying pan, add the meatballs and fry over a medium heat, turning until evenly browned but not cooked through. Drain and transfer to the slow cooker pot.

Make the sauce. Add the butter and onion to a clean frying pan. Fry, stirring, for 5 minutes or until the onion is softened and just beginning to turn golden. Stir in the flour, then gradually mix in the stock and bring to the boil, stirring. Season with salt and pepper and pour the sauce over the meatballs. Cover with the lid and cook on low for 6–8 hours.

Stir the chopped dill into the sauce and serve the meatballs with mashed potato sprinkled with a little extra chopped dill to garnish.

Short-cut suppers

The beauty of slow cooking is that you can get supper on the go before leaving for work or a trip out. If you have to make an early start in the morning you can part-prepare the recipes in this chapter the night before, then put the ingredients into the slow cooker with hot liquid.

*B*arley risotto
with blue cheese butter

175 g (6 oz) pearl barley

1 onion, finely chopped

2 garlic cloves, finely chopped

500 g (1 lb) butternut squash,
    peeled, deseeded and cut into
    1.5 cm (¾ inch) pieces

1 litre (1¾ pints) boiling vegetable
    stock

125 g (4 oz) baby spinach, washed
    and well drained

BLUE CHEESE BUTTER

100 g (3½ oz) butter at room
    temperature

100 g (3½ oz) blue cheese,
    rind removed

1 garlic clove, finely chopped

¼ teaspoon crushed dried red chillies

salt and pepper

Preheat the slow cooker if necessary; see the manufacturer's handbook. Put the pearl barley, onion, garlic and butternut squash in the slow cooker pot. Add the stock and a little salt and pepper. Cover with the lid and cook on low for 6–8 hours or until the barley and squash are tender.

Meanwhile, make the blue cheese butter. Put the butter on a plate, crumble the cheese on top, add the garlic and chillies and mash together with a fork. Spoon the butter into a line on a piece of nonstick baking paper, then wrap it in paper and roll it backwards and forwards to make a neat sausage shape. Chill until required.

When almost ready to serve, stir the risotto, slice half the butter and add to the slow cooker pot. Mix together until just beginning to melt, then add the spinach. Replace the lid and cook, still on low, for 15 minutes until the spinach has just wilted. Ladle into shallow bowls and serve topped with slices of the remaining butter.

To save time in the morning, put the barley, vegetables and garlic in a clingfilm-wrapped bowl in the refrigerator and prepare the butter the night before. The next day, crumble a stock cube into a jug of boiling water and add everything to the slow cooker.

Chicken & mascarpone
pasta bake

500 g (1 lb) boneless, skinless chicken thighs, cut into chunks

1 onion, finely chopped

1 red and 1 orange pepper, cored, deseeded and diced

6 sun-dried tomatoes in oil, drained and sliced

2 garlic cloves, finely chopped

1 tablespoon cornflour

400 g (13 oz) can chopped tomatoes

1 chicken stock cube

250 ml (8 fl oz) water

300 g (10 oz) penne

75 g (3 oz) mascarpone cheese

small bunch of basil

salt and pepper

Preheat the slow cooker if necessary; see the manufacturer's handbook. Put the chicken, onion, peppers, sun-dried tomatoes and garlic into the slow cooker. Mix the cornflour in a small bowl with a little water to make a smooth paste and add this to the slow cooker.

Pour the tomatoes into a microproof measuring jug, crumble in the stock cube, add the water and cook on full power for $2^1/_2$ minutes until piping hot. Season with salt and pepper and pour into the slow cooker pot.

Mix together, then cover with the lid and cook on high for 30 minutes. Reduce to low and cook for $7^1/_2$–$9^1/_2$ hours or set to auto for 8–10 hours.

When almost ready to serve, add the pasta to a saucepan of boiling water and cook for 8–10 minutes until just tender. Stir the mascarpone cheese into the chicken with half the basil leaves.

Drain the pasta and stir into the sauce. Spoon into shallow bowls and serve sprinkled with the remaining basil leaves.

Mascarpone cheese adds a wonderful creaminess to this garlicky tomato sauce, but you could stir in a garlic and herb full-fat cream cheese or a few tablespoons of double cream if you don't have any mascarpone.

$\mathscr{S}$moked cod
with cannellini bean mash

2 x 410 g (13½ oz) cans cannellini
  beans, drained

1 bunch of spring onions, thinly
  sliced; white and green parts
  kept separate

400 ml (14 fl oz) boiling fish stock

1 teaspoon wholegrain mustard

grated rind and juice of 1 lemon

4 smoked cod loins, about 625 g
  (1¼ lb) in total

4 tablespoons full-fat crème fraîche

small bunch of parsley, watercress or
  rocket leaves, roughly chopped

salt and pepper

Preheat the slow cooker if necessary; see the manufacturer's handbook. Add the drained beans to the slow cooker with the white onion slices. Mix the fish stock with the mustard, lemon rind and juice and a little salt and pepper, then pour into the slow cooker pot.

Arrange the fish on top and sprinkle with a little extra pepper. Cover with the lid and cook on low for 1½–2 hours or until the fish flakes easily when pressed in the centre with a knife.

Remove the fish with a slotted spoon and transfer to a plate. Pour off nearly all the cooking liquid, then mash the beans roughly. Stir in the crème fraîche, the remaining onion and the parsley, watercress or rocket. Taste and adjust the seasoning if needed. Spoon the mash on to plates and top with the fish.

Most of us don't have time to make homemade stock, so make up a low-salt stock cube with boiling water from the kettle, making sure it has completely dissolved, then add the liquid directly to the slow cooker pot.

PREPARATION TIME **25 minutes, plus marinating**

COOKING TEMPERATURE **high and low**

COOKING TIME **10–11 hours**

SERVES **4**

 Stifado

200 ml (7 fl oz) red wine

1 tablespoon tomato purée

2 tablespoons olive oil

2–3 stems of thyme or bay leaves

4 cloves

¼ teaspoon ground allspice

300 g (10 oz) shallots, halved if large

2 garlic cloves, finely chopped

750 g (1½ lb) stewing beef, cut into large chunks and any fat discarded

4 teaspoons cornflour

150 ml (¼ pint) cold water

½ stock cube

salt and pepper

TO SERVE

toasted, sliced French bread

herb butter

The night before, mix the wine, tomato purée and oil in a shallow, non-metallic dish. Add the herbs, spices and some salt and pepper and mix together. Then add the shallots and garlic. Add the beef, toss in the marinade, cover with clingfilm and chill overnight in the refrigerator.

Preheat the slow cooker if necessary; see the manufacturer's handbook. Put the cornflour in a saucepan, mix in a little of the water to make a smooth paste, then mix in the remaining water. Drain the marinade from the beef into the pan and crumble in the stock cube. Bring to the boil, stirring.

Tip the beef, shallots and flavourings into the slow cooker pot, pour over the hot stock mixture, cover with the lid and cook on high for 30 minutes. Reduce to low and cook for 9½–10½ hours or set to auto for 10–11 hours until the meat is tender.

Spoon into bowls and serve with toasted French bread spread with a herb butter.

 This aromatic Greek stew was traditionally cooked overnight in an outdoor clay oven, making it an ideal recipe to adapt for the slow cooker. The marinade may also be used for rabbit or chicken portions.

Moroccan lamb

1 onion, thinly sliced

2 carrots, diced

250 g (8 oz) swede, diced

4 cm (1¹/₂ inch) fresh root ginger, peeled and finely chopped

grated rind of 1 lemon

2 teaspoons harissa (Moroccan chilli paste)

¹/₂ teaspoon ground allspice

675 g (1 lb 6 oz) lamb rump or shoulder steaks

1 tablespoon cornflour

400 g (13 oz) can chopped tomatoes

150 ml (¹/₄ pint) lamb stock

salt and pepper

lemon wedges, to garnish

TO SERVE

couscous

pitta bread

Preheat the slow cooker if necessary; see the manufacturer's handbook. Put the onion and diced vegetables into the slow cooker pot, add the ginger, lemon rind, harissa and allspice and arrange the lamb steaks on top.

Mix the cornflour to a smooth paste with a little water in a small bowl. Put the tomatoes and stock in a saucepan, mix in the cornflour paste and some salt and pepper and bring to the boil; alternatively, heat in a microwave if you prefer. Pour over the lamb.

Cover with the lid and cook on high for 30 minutes. Reduce to low and cook for 7¹/₂–9¹/₂ hours or set to auto for 8–10 hours or until the lamb is tender. Garnish with lemon wedges and serve with couscous tossed with the juice of 1 lemon and toasted pitta bread.

The vegetables, ginger and lemon rind can be prepared the night before and put into a plastic bag in the refrigerator. If you really like garlic, add 2 finely chopped garlic cloves or add some ready-prepared garlic purée from a jar.

Tomato braised squid
with chorizo

625 g (1¼ lb) chilled squid

1 onion, thinly sliced

125 g (4 oz) ready-diced chorizo

125 g (4 oz) closed-cup mushrooms, sliced

1 red pepper, cored, deseeded and sliced

2 garlic cloves, finely chopped

2–3 sprigs of rosemary, leaves stripped from the stems

1 tablespoon tomato purée

1 teaspoon caster sugar

400 g (13 oz) can chopped tomatoes

100 ml (3½ fl oz) red wine

1 tablespoon cornflour

salt and pepper

chopped parsley, to garnish

rice or thickly sliced bread, to serve

Preheat the slow cooker if necessary; see the manufacturer's handbook. Rinse the squid inside and out, pulling out the tentacles and reserving. Drain and slice the bodies. Put the tentacles in a bowl, cover with clingfilm and refrigerate.

Put the onion, chorizo, mushrooms and red pepper in the slow cooker pot. Add the garlic, rosemary, tomato purée and sugar, then stir in the sliced squid.

Pour the tomatoes and wine into a saucepan and bring to the boil; alternatively, heat in a microwave if you prefer. Add a little salt and pepper, then pour the mixture into the slow cooker pot and stir all ingredients together.

Cover with the lid and cook on low for 3–5 hours or until the squid is tender.

When almost ready to serve, mix the cornflour to a paste with a little water in a small bowl. Stir into the slow cooker pot, add the squid tentacles, then replace the lid and cook on low for 30 minutes. Spoon the squid mixture into bowls lined with rice and serve sprinkled with chopped parsley, or serve with thickly sliced bread instead.

The secret of succulent squid is to cook it either very fast in a frying pan or very slowly, as here, with wine and tomatoes. The chorizo adds a depth and spiciness to the sauce.

Chicken avgolemono

8 boneless, skinless chicken thighs, about 700 g (1 lb 6 oz) in total

1 onion, thinly sliced

2–3 stems of oregano or basil

450 ml (³/₄ pint) boiling chicken stock

grated rind and juice of 1 lemon

300 g (10 oz) macaroni or orzo pasta

2 whole eggs

2 egg yolks

4 tablespoons chopped parsley, plus extra to garnish (optional)

salt and pepper

lemon rind curls, to garnish (optional)

Preheat the slow cooker if necessary; see the manufacturer's handbook. Put the chicken, onion and oregano or basil into the slow cooker pot. Mix the stock with the lemon rind and juice and some salt and pepper. Pour the liquid over the chicken.

Cover with the lid and cook on high for 30 minutes. Reduce to low and cook for 5¹/₂–6¹/₂ hours or set to auto for 6–8 hours or until the chicken is tender.

When almost ready to serve, bring a large saucepan of water to the boil, add the pasta and cook for 9–10 minutes until just tender.

Meanwhile, drain the stock from the slow cooker into a second large saucepan and boil for 5 minutes until reduced by one-third or to about 200 ml (7 fl oz).

Whisk the eggs and egg yolks in a bowl, then gradually whisk in 2 ladlefuls of stock until smooth. Pour into the saucepan with the remaining stock, then whisk over a gentle heat until the sauce has thickened slightly. Stir in the parsley and check the seasoning.

Pour the sauce over the chicken. Spoon the pasta into shallow serving bowls and top with the chicken. Garnish with lemon rind curls and extra chopped parsley, if liked.

This simple sauce is easy to make, but it will need some careful watching while the eggs are cooking, as if it boils it will curdle in the same way as a sweet custard sauce.

Gammon in cola

1.25 kg (2½ lb) boneless smoked gammon joint, soaked overnight in cold water

5 cloves

1 onion, cut into 8 wedges

2 carrots, thickly sliced

410 g (13½ oz) can black beans or red kidney beans, drained

2 bay leaves

900 ml (1½ pints) cola

1 tablespoon dark muscovado sugar

1 tablespoon tomato purée

2 teaspoons English mustard

Preheat the slow cooker if necessary; see the manufacturer's handbook. Drain the gammon joint and put it into the slow cooker pot. Press the cloves into 5 of the onion wedges and add to the gammon with the remaining onion wedges and carrot slices. Tip in the drained beans and add the bay leaves.

Pour the cola into a saucepan, add the sugar, tomato purée and mustard and bring to the boil, stirring. Pour over the gammon, cover with the lid and cook on high for 6–7 hours or until the gammon is tender.

Strain the cooking liquid into a saucepan and boil rapidly for 10 minutes to reduce by half. Keep the gammon and vegetables hot in the turned-off slow cooker with the lid on.

Slice the gammon thinly and arrange on plates with the vegetables, beans and a drizzle of sauce.

*B*oston baked beans

1 onion, finely chopped

2 carrots, diced

410 g (13^1/$_2$ oz) can black eye beans, drained

410 g (13^1/$_2$ oz) can borlotti beans, drained

2 bay leaves

2 teaspoons English mustard

1 tablespoon cornflour

1 tablespoon black treacle

2 tablespoons tomato purée

2 tablespoons light muscovado sugar

2 tablespoons malt or red wine vinegar

1 chicken stock cube

450 ml (^{3}/$_4$ pint) boiling water

750 g (1^1/$_2$ lb) rindless belly pork slices

salt and pepper

garlic or herb bread, to serve (optional)

Preheat the slow cooker if necessary; see the manufacturer's handbook. Add the onion, carrots, drained beans and bay leaves to the slow cooker pot and mix together.

In a bowl mix together the mustard, cornflour, treacle, tomato purée, sugar and vinegar. Crumble in the stock cube, then gradually mix in the boiling water. Tip into the slow cooker and stir together.

Add the belly pork slices in a single layer and press beneath the level of the liquid. Cover with the lid and cook on high for 30 minutes. Reduce to low and cook for 7^1/$_2$–9^1/$_2$ hours or set to auto for 8–10 hours. Serve with hot garlic or herb bread, if liked.

Canned beans have been used here to save time, but you can also use dried ones. Soak them overnight in plenty of cold water, then bring to the boil in a pan of fresh water. Boil rapidly for 10 minutes, then drain and add to the slow cooker pot.

PREPARATION TIME **15 minutes**

COOKING TEMPERATURE **high**

COOKING TIME **1¹/₂–2 hours**

SERVES **4**

$\mathcal{H}$ot soused herring

1 large red onion, thinly sliced

1 large carrot, cut into matchsticks

1 large celery stick, thinly sliced

6 small herrings, gutted, filleted and
  rinsed with cold water

2 stems of tarragon, plus extra sprigs
  to garnish

1 bay leaf

150 ml (¹/₄ pint) cider vinegar

25 g (1 oz) caster sugar

600 ml (1 pint) boiling water

¹/₂ teaspoon mixed peppercorns

salt

Preheat the slow cooker if necessary; see the manufacturer's handbook. Put half the onion, carrot and celery in the slow cooker pot. Arrange the herring fillets on top, then cover them with the remaining vegetables.

Add the tarragon, bay leaf, vinegar and sugar. Pour over the boiling water and add the peppercorns and a little salt. Cover with the lid and cook on high for 1¹/₂–2 hours or until the fish flakes when pressed with a knife.

Spoon the fish, vegetables and a little of the cooking liquid into shallow bowls, halving the fish fillets, if liked. Garnish with tarragon sprigs. Serve with pickled beetroot, dill cucumbers and bread and butter, if liked.

$\mathcal{P}$ork goulash

1 onion, finely chopped

250 g (8 oz) red cabbage,
 finely shredded and woody
 core discarded

1 teaspoon caraway seeds

1 teaspoon paprika

$\frac{1}{4}$ teaspoon ground allspice

$\frac{1}{2}$ teaspoon crushed dried red chillies

4 teaspoons cornflour

1 tablespoon light muscovado sugar

2 tablespoons tomato purée

2 tablespoons red wine vinegar

4 pork loin chops, about 1 kg (2 lb)
 in total

400 ml (14 fl oz) boiling chicken
 stock

salt and pepper

garlic bread, to serve (optional)

TO GARNISH

soured cream

paprika

crushed dried red chillies

Preheat the slow cooker if necessary; see the manufacturer's handbook. Put the onion and red cabbage into the slow cooker pot. Mix the seeds, spices and chilli in a small bowl with the cornflour, sugar, tomato purée and vinegar. Put the pork chops on top of the cabbage and pour the spice mix on top.

Pour over the stock, add a little salt and pepper, then cover and cook on high for 30 minutes. Reduce to low and cook for $7\frac{1}{2}$–$9\frac{1}{2}$ hours or set to auto for 8–10 hours or until the pork and cabbage are tender.

Spoon the goulash into shallow bowls, top with spoonfuls of soured cream and a sprinkling of paprika and extra chilli. Serve with garlic bread, if liked.

Forgotten cuts

The old-fashioned cuts our grandmothers used to cook are making a trendy comeback. They're cheap and readily available, and they taste better the longer they cook, making them perfect for your slow cooker.

Pot-roast beef
with brown ale

1 kg (2 lb) beef brisket

2–3 stems of rosemary

8 rashers smoked streaky bacon

25 g (1 oz) butter

2 tablespoons plain flour

300 ml (½ pint) brown ale

300 ml (½ pint) beef stock

2 teaspoons wholegrain mustard

1 tablespoon tomato purée

4 baby parsnips, quartered

250 g (8 oz) chantenay carrots, any
large ones halved

1 leek, thickly sliced

salt and pepper

crusty bread, to serve (optional)

Preheat the slow cooker if necessary; see the manufacturer's handbook. Remove the string from the beef, tuck the rosemary into the centre, then wrap the sides with the bacon and tie in place with fresh string.

Heat the butter in a frying pan, add the beef and fry the bacon-wrapped edges until they are browned. Transfer the beef to the slow cooker pot. Stir the flour into the pan juices, then mix in the ale, stock, mustard and tomato purée. Add a little salt and pepper and bring to the boil, stirring.

Pour the mixture over the beef, add the vegetables and press beneath the surface of the liquid. Cover and cook on high for 5–6 hours or until the vegetables are tender.

Lift the beef on to a chopping board and cut it into thin slices, discarding the string and rosemary stems. Arrange in shallow serving bowls and add the vegetables and a ladleful of beery juices to each one. Serve with warm crusty bread for dunking, if liked.

Brisket has a coarser texture than more traditional roasting joints, so carve it into thin slices and serve with lots of the cooking juices. Any leftover cooking juices make a great base for a soup with extra vegetables or a mix of vegetables and lentils.

Stuffed breast of lamb

1 breast of lamb, about 750 g (1½ lb)

400 g (13 oz) speciality flavoured sausages such as Toulouse or Sicilian

75 g (3 oz) ready-to-eat dried apricots, chopped

1 tablespoon olive oil

1 onion, sliced

2 tablespoons plain flour

450 ml (¾ pint) lamb stock

2–3 stems of rosemary

1 tablespoon tomato purée

salt and pepper

TO SERVE

rice

green beans

Preheat the slow cooker if necessary; see the manufacturer's handbook. Remove the string from the breast of lamb and open it out flat on a chopping board. Cut along the length of each sausage and peel off the skin. Press the sausagemeat over the lamb and sprinkle over the chopped apricots. Roll up the lamb and tie at intervals with string.

Heat the oil in a frying pan, add the lamb and brown on all sides, adding the onions halfway through and frying these until softened.

Transfer the lamb to the slow cooker pot. Stir the flour into the onion, then mix in the stock, rosemary, tomato purée and a little salt and pepper. Bring to the boil and pour over the lamb.

Cover with the lid and cook on high for 6–7 hours or until the lamb is very tender. Cut into 8 slices, discarding the string, and serve in shallow bowls on a bed of rice with green beans, spooning the cooking juices around.

This is an excellent budget-friendly roast. Breast of lamb is extremely cheap and mixed with gourmet flavoured sausages it easily serves four hungry people. It is also delicious served on a bed of mixed root mash or mashed sweet potato with chopped chilli.

PREPARATION TIME **30 minutes**

COOKING TEMPERATURE **high**

COOKING TIME **6–7 hours**

SERVES **4**

Turkey tagine

1 turkey drumstick, about 700 g
    (1 lb 6 oz)

1 tablespoon olive oil

1 onion, chopped

2 garlic cloves, finely chopped

2.5 cm (1 inch) fresh root ginger,
    peeled and finely chopped

2 tablespoons plain flour

1 teaspoon turmeric

1 teaspoon ground cinnamon

1 teaspoon ground coriander

$^1/_2$ teaspoon cumin seeds

600 ml (1 pint) boiling chicken stock

410 g ($13^1/_2$ oz) can chickpeas,
    drained

200 g (7 oz) parsnips, diced

200 g (7 oz) carrots, diced

salt and pepper

small bunch of coriander,
    roughly chopped

TO SERVE

rice or couscous

naan bread

Check that the turkey drumstick will fit into the slow cooker pot before you begin, cutting off the knuckle end if needed with a large knife and hitting it with a rolling pin or hammer to sever. Preheat the slow cooker if necessary; see the manufacturer's handbook.

Heat the oil in a frying pan, add the drumstick and fry, turning, until golden-brown all over. Transfer to the slow cooker pot. Add the onion to the pan and fry until softened. Stir in the garlic, ginger and flour, then mix in the spices. Gradually stir in the stock, season to taste with salt and pepper and bring to the boil.

Pour the onion mixture over the turkey. Add the chickpeas and vegetables to the pot and press beneath the stock. Cover with the lid and cook on high for 6–7 hours or until the meat is tender and almost falling off the bone.

Lift the turkey drumstick out of the slow cooker pot and take the meat off the bone, discarding the skin and tendons. Cut it into bite-sized pieces and return them to the slow cooker pot. Stir in the chopped coriander and serve with rice or couscous and naan bread.

Turkey drumsticks are a good-value cut and needn't be thought of as something to eat only at Thanksgiving or Christmas time. Sold all the year round in supermarkets, they really suit long, slow cooking and can be mixed with Moroccan or Indian spice blends.

PREPARATION TIME **15 minutes**

COOKING TEMPERATURE **low**

COOKING TIME **9–10 hours**

SERVES **4**

Oxtail bredie

1–2 tablespoons sunflower oil

1 kg (2 lb) oxtail

2 onions, sliced

2.5 cm (1 inch) fresh root ginger,
  peeled and finely chopped

$\frac{1}{2}$ teaspoon dried crushed red chillies

$\frac{1}{2}$ teaspoon ground cinnamon

1 teaspoon ground cumin

2 tablespoons plain flour

400 g (13 oz) can chopped tomatoes

300 ml ($\frac{1}{2}$ pint) beef stock

2 bay leaves

2 tablespoons light muscovado sugar

2 tablespoons malt vinegar

salt and pepper

chopped parsley or coriander,
  to garnish

mashed sweet potatoes, to serve

Preheat the slow cooker if necessary; see the manufacturer's handbook. Heat 1 tablespoon of the oil in a frying pan, add the oxtail and fry until browned on all sides. Lift it out of the pan with a slotted spoon and put it into the slow cooker pot.

Add the onion to the pan with a little extra oil and fry for 5 minutes until softened and lightly browned. Stir in the ginger, chillies and ground spices, then add the flour. Gradually mix in the tomatoes and stock. Stir in the bay leaves, sugar, vinegar and a little salt and pepper.

Bring the mixture to the boil, spoon into the slow cooker pot, cover and cook on low for 9–10 hours or until the oxtail is tender and almost falling off the bones. Serve scooped on to mashed sweet potatoes and sprinkled with a little chopped parsley or coriander.

There are many versions of this tomato-based bredie, the Afrikaans name for a South African tomato stew. They are mostly made with mutton, but the cinnamon, chilli and sweet, slightly sour sauce also compliment the richness of oxtail.

PREPARATION TIME **20 minutes**

COOKING TEMPERATURE **low**

COOKING TIME **6–7 hours**

SERVES **4**

$\mathcal{N}$ ormandy rabbit

2 tablespoons plain flour

1 rabbit, cut into 4 pieces

1 tablespoon olive oil

25 g (1 oz) butter

1 large onion, sliced

2 sharp dessert apples, such as
   Granny Smith, cored and
   quartered

3 tablespoons Calvados or brandy

250 ml (8 fl oz) chicken stock

150 ml (¼ pint) Normandy cider

3 teaspoons wholegrain mustard

4 tablespoons crème fraîche
   (optional)

salt and pepper

TO SERVE

sugar snap peas

baby new potatoes

parsley

Preheat the slow cooker if necessary; see the manufacturer's handbook. Put the flour on a plate, mix with a little salt and pepper and use it to dust the rabbit pieces all over.

Heat the oil and butter in a frying pan, add the rabbit pieces and brown on both sides. Lift out and transfer to the slow cooker pot.

Add the onion to the pan and fry, stirring, until lightly browned. Add the apples and Calvados or brandy and bring to the boil. Light the brandy with a long taper and stand well back until the flames subside.

Mix in the stock, cider, mustard and a little salt and pepper. Bring to the boil, then pour over the rabbit. Cover with the lid and cook on low for 6–7 hours. Stir the sauce. Mix in the crème fraîche (if used) and serve with sugar snap peas and roughly crushed baby new potatoes mixed with a little chopped parsley.

Rabbit goes well with cider and brandy in this Normandy version of *coq au vin*. You can use chicken thigh and leg joints instead, or try the recipe with 8 large pork sausages, but omit the flaming Calvados or brandy stage and serve without the crème fraîche.

*A*lsace-style pork

1 tablespoon sunflower oil

1 onion, chopped

1 dessert apple, cored and diced

4 tomatoes, diced

1 teaspoon caraway seeds

300 ml (½ pint) blond beer or lager

150 ml (¼ pint) chicken stock

375 g (12 oz) sauerkraut, drained

1 kg (2 lb) large pork hock

4 dried pork kabanos sausages, about
   125 g (4 oz), halved

2 carrots, diced

2–3 pickled dill cucumbers, about
   125 g (4 oz) sliced

salt and pepper

chopped parsley, to garnish

rye bread, to serve (optional)

Preheat the slow cooker if necessary; see the manufacturer's handbook. Heat the oil in a frying pan, add the onion and fry, stirring, for 5 minutes or until softened. Add the apple, tomatoes, caraway seeds, beer and stock. Season with salt and pepper and bring to the boil.

Tip into the slow cooker pot, add the drained sauerkraut and stir together. Press the pork hock into the centre, then add the sausages, carrots and dill cucumbers and press into the liquid. Cover with the lid and cook on high for 6–7 hours.

Sprinkle the hock with chopped parsley and serve straight from the pot or lift it out of the slow cooker, take off the skin and remove the bone. Cut the meat into bite-sized pieces and spoon back into the slow cooker. Sprinkle with parsley and serve in shallow bowls topped with the sauce and accompanied with rye bread, if liked.

Cut from the hand and spring,
a pork hock is the lower part of
the leg, and you will need to ask
the butcher to cut it for you.
Any leftover gravy will set to
a jelly when it is cold.

*H*am hock with lentils
& chillied squash

1–1.25 kg (2–2½ lb) smoked bacon
    hock, soaked overnight in cold
    water

200 g (7 oz) Puy lentils

2 small onions, cut into thick wedges

1 small butternut squash, cut into
    4–6 slices and seeds scooped out
    (leave the skin on)

2 bay leaves

1 teaspoon fennel seeds

½–¾ teaspoon crushed dried
    red chillies

750 ml (1¼ pints) boiling water

pepper

small bunch of parsley, roughly
    chopped, to garnish (optional)

Preheat the slow cooker if necessary; see the manufacturer's handbook.
Drain the gammon joint and put it in the slow cooker pot. Add the
lentils, onions and squash. Add the bay leaves, sprinkle over the fennel
seeds, chillies and a little pepper, then pour in the boiling water.

Cover with the lid and cook on high for 6–7 hours or until the gammon
is tender and the lentils are soft.

Lift the gammon out of the slow cooker pot and put it on a serving dish.
Peel away the rind and remove the bone, then cut the meat into chunks.
Spoon the lentils and vegetables into shallow bowls, then top with the
ham. Sprinkle with the parsley, if liked, and serve the remaining
cooking juices ladled into a jug or bowl for diners to add as required.

**Leaving the squash skin in place during
cooking stops the flesh from falling apart,
but if you can't get a small butternut squash,
cut 500 g (1 lb) from a larger one and cut
it into 4 pieces. Bacon hocks can be salty
so add salt to taste at the very end.**

$\mathcal{N}$avarin of lamb
with spring vegetables

1 tablespoon olive oil

1 kg (2 lb) neck of lamb or a
  supermarket pack of mixed
  stewing lamb pieces

400 g (13 oz) baby new potatoes,
  scrubbed and halved if large

250 g (8 oz) shallots, halved if large

2 garlic cloves, finely chopped
  (optional)

2 tablespoons plain flour

600 ml (1 pint) lamb stock

2 teaspoons tomato purée

1 teaspoon Dijon mustard

1 fresh or dried bouquet garni

salt and pepper

TO FINISH

75 g (3 oz) green beans, halved

100 g (3½ oz) thin asparagus spears,
  stems halved

75 g (3 oz) frozen broad beans
  or peas

3 tablespoons chopped parsley
  (optional)

Preheat the slow cooker if necessary; see the manufacturer's handbook.
Heat the oil in a frying pan, add the lamb pieces and fry until browned
on both sides. Lift out of pan with a slotted spoon and add to the slow
cooker pot with the potatoes.

Add the shallots and garlic (if used) to the frying pan, fry until lightly
browned, then stir in the flour. Gradually mix in the stock. Add the
tomato purée, mustard, bouquet garni and a little salt and pepper.
Bring to the boil, then pour over the lamb.

Cover with the lid and cook on high for 6–7 hours until the lamb
is tender. Just before serving put the green vegetables in a small
saucepan of boiling water. Simmer for 5 minutes, then drain and toss
with the parsley (if used). Stir the lamb and spoon the vegetables on
top. Serve in shallow bowls.

Neck of lamb is incredibly cheap, and when
it's cooked for a long time it practically falls
off the bone. You might prefer to take the
meat off the bones before serving, especially
if you have young children, or you could use
4 small lamb shanks instead.

Vegetarian

You can do a lot more in your slow cooker than just making meaty casseroles. Try these vegetarian main meals and accompaniments flavoured with spices from around the world. And remember: you don't have to make them just for your vegetarian friends.

PREPARATION TIME **30 minutes**

COOKING TEMPERATURE **low and high**

COOKING TIME **6³/₄–8³/₄ hours**

SERVES **4**

*M*ushroom cobbler

2 tablespoons olive oil

1 onion, chopped

2 garlic cloves, chopped

250 g (8 oz) flat mushrooms,
    peeled and quartered

250 g (8 oz) cup chestnut
    mushrooms, quartered

1 tablespoon plain flour

200 ml (7 fl oz) red wine

400 g (13 oz) can chopped tomatoes

150 ml (¹/₄ pint) vegetable stock

1 tablespoon redcurrant jelly

2–3 stems of thyme

salt and pepper

WALNUT SCONES

200 g (7 oz) self-raising flour

50 g (2 oz) butter, diced

50 g (2 oz) walnut pieces, chopped

75 g (3 oz) Cheddar cheese, grated

1 egg, beaten

4–5 tablespoons milk

Preheat the slow cooker if necessary; see the manufacturer's handbook. Heat the oil in a frying pan, add the onion, garlic and mushrooms and fry, stirring, for 5 minutes or until just turning golden.

Stir in the flour, then mix in the wine, tomatoes and stock. Add the redcurrant jelly, thyme and salt and pepper and bring to the boil. Pour into the slow cooker pot, cover with the lid and cook on low for 6–8 hours.

When almost ready to serve, make the topping. Put the flour and butter in a bowl, rub in the butter with your fingertips until the mixture resembles fine breadcrumbs. Stir in the walnuts, Cheddar and salt and pepper. Add half the egg, then mix in enough milk to make a soft dough.

Knead lightly, then roll out the dough on a lightly floured surface until 2 cm (³/₄ inch) thick. Stamp out 8 rounds with a 6 cm (2¹/₂ inch) plain biscuit cutter, re-rolling the trimmings as needed. Stir the mushroom casserole, then arrange the scones, slightly overlapping, around the edge of the dish. Cover with the lid and cook on high for 45 minutes or until well risen.

Lift the pot out of the housing using oven gloves, brush the tops of the scones with the remaining egg and brown under a preheated hot grill, if liked.

$\mathscr{A}$ubergine ratatouille
with ricotta dumplings

3 tablespoons olive oil

1 onion, chopped

1 aubergine, sliced

2 courgettes, about 375 g (12 oz) in total, sliced

1 red pepper, cored, deseeded and diced

1 yellow pepper, cored, deseeded and diced

2 garlic cloves, finely chopped

1 tablespoon plain flour

400 g (13 oz) can chopped tomatoes

300 ml (½ pint) vegetable stock

2–3 stems of rosemary

salt and pepper

DUMPLINGS

100 g (3½ oz) plain flour

75 g (3 oz) ricotta cheese

grated rind of ½ lemon

1 egg, beaten

Preheat the slow cooker if necessary; see the manufacturer's handbook. Heat the oil in a frying pan, add the onion and aubergine and fry, stirring, for 5 minutes or until softened and beginning to turn golden.

Stir in the courgettes, peppers and garlic and fry for 3–4 minutes. Mix in the flour, then the tomatoes, stock, rosemary and a little salt and pepper. Bring to the boil, then spoon into the slow cooker pot. Cover with the lid and cook on high for 3–4 hours until the vegetables are tender.

When almost ready to serve, make the dumplings. Put the flour, ricotta, lemon rind and a little salt and pepper into a bowl. Add the egg and mix to a soft but not sticky dough. Cut into 12 pieces and roll each piece into a ball with floured hands.

Stir the ratatouille and arrange the dumplings on the top. Replace the lid and cook for 15–20 minutes or until the dumplings are light and firm to the touch.

These lemon-flavoured Italian inspired dumplings also taste good added to slow-cooked root vegetable soups or added to more robust mushroom and lentil stews, and even in chillied bean mixtures.

$\mathcal{A}$romatic sweet potato
& egg curry

1 tablespoon sunflower oil

1 onion, chopped

1 teaspoon cumin seeds, roughly crushed

1 teaspoon ground coriander

1 teaspoon turmeric

1 teaspoon garam masala

1/2 teaspoon crushed dried red chillies

300 g (10 oz) sweet potatoes, diced

2 garlic cloves, finely chopped

400 g (13 oz) can chopped tomatoes

410 g (13 1/2 oz) can lentils, drained

300 ml (1/2 pint) vegetable stock

1 teaspoon caster sugar

6 eggs

150 g (5 oz) frozen peas

150 ml (1/4 pint) double cream

small bunch of coriander, torn into pieces

salt and pepper

rice or naan bread, to serve (optional)

Preheat the slow cooker if necessary; see the manufacturer's handbook. Heat the oil in a frying pan, add the onion and fry, stirring, for 5 minutes or until softened and just beginning to turn golden.

Stir in the spices, dried chillies, sweet potatoes and garlic and fry for 2 minutes. Add the tomatoes, lentils, stock and sugar and season with a little salt and pepper. Bring to the boil, stirring. Spoon into the slow cooker pot, cover with the lid and cook on low for 6–8 hours.

When almost ready to serve, put the eggs in a small saucepan, cover with cold water, bring to the boil and simmer for 8 minutes. Drain, crack the shells and cool under cold running water. Peel and halve the eggs, then add to the slow cooker pot with the peas, cream and half the coriander. Cover with the lid and cook on low for 15 minutes.

Spoon the curry into bowls, garnish with the remaining coriander and serve with rice or warm naan bread, if liked.

Courgette tian

50 g (2 oz) long-grain rice

butter, for greasing

1 tomato, sliced

1 tablespoon olive oil

½ onion, chopped

1 garlic clove, finely chopped

1 courgette, about 175 g (6 oz),
  coarsely grated

125 g (4 oz) spinach, thickly
  shredded

3 eggs

6 tablespoons milk

pinch of grated nutmeg

4 tablespoons chopped mint

salt and pepper

Preheat the slow cooker if necessary; see the manufacturer's handbook. Bring a small saucepan of water to the boil, add the rice, bring back to the boil, then simmer for 8–10 minutes or until tender. Meanwhile, butter the inside of a soufflé dish that is 14 cm (5½ inches) in diameter and 9 cm (3½ inches) high. Base-line with nonstick baking paper, and arrange the tomato slices, overlapping, on the paper.

Heat the oil in a frying pan, add the onion and fry, stirring, for 5 minutes or until softened and just beginning to turn golden. Stir in the garlic, then add the courgette and spinach and cook for 2 minutes or until the spinach is just wilted.

Beat together the eggs, milk, nutmeg and a little salt and pepper. Drain the rice and stir into the spinach mixture with the egg mixture and mint. Mix well, then spoon into the dish. Cover loosely with buttered foil and lower into the slow cooker pot with foil straps (see page 17) or tie string around the top edge.

Pour boiling water into the slow cooker pot to come halfway up the sides of the dish. Cover with the lid and cook on high for 1½–2 hours or until the tian is set in the middle. Lift out of the slow cooker and leave to stand for 5 minutes.

Remove the foil from the tian, loosen the edge and turn it out on to a plate. Peel off the lining paper, cut into wedges and serve warm with salad, if liked.

Balsamic tomatoes
with spaghetti

1 tablespoon olive oil

750 g (1½ lb) plum tomatoes, halved

4 tablespoons white wine

4 teaspoons good balsamic vinegar

375 g (12 oz) spaghetti

salt and pepper

TO GARNISH

small bunch of basil

freshly grated or shaved Parmesan
  cheese

Preheat the slow cooker if necessary; see the manufacturer's handbook. Brush the oil over the base of the slow cooker pot, add the tomatoes, cut side down, drizzle over the wine and vinegar and add a little salt and pepper. Cover with the lid and cook on high for 3–4 hours.

When almost ready to serve, bring a large saucepan of water to the boil, add the pasta and cook for 6–7 minutes or until tender. Drain and mix into the sauce.

Spoon the pasta into bowls and serve sprinkled with basil leaves and grated or shaved Parmesan.

If you prefer a thicker tomato sauce mix a few teaspoons of cornflour to a paste with some cold water and stir the mixture into the sauce 30 minutes before the end of cooking.

PREPARATION TIME **20 minutes**

COOKING TEMPERATURE **low**

COOKING TIME **4–5 hours**

SERVES **4**

$\mathcal{H}$erby stuffed peppers

4 different coloured peppers

100 g (3½ oz) easy-cook brown rice

410 g (13½ oz) can chickpeas, drained

small bunch of parsley, roughly chopped

small bunch of mint, roughly chopped

1 onion, finely chopped

2 garlic cloves, finely chopped

½ teaspoon smoked paprika (pimenton)

1 teaspoon ground allspice

600 ml (1 pint) hot vegetable stock

salt and pepper

Preheat the slow cooker if necessary; see the manufacturer's handbook. Cut the top off each pepper and remove the core and seeds.

Mix together the rice, chickpeas, herbs, onion, garlic, paprika and allspice with plenty of salt and pepper. Spoon the mixture into the peppers, then put the peppers into the slow cooker pot.

Pour the hot stock around the peppers, cover with the lid and cook on low for 4–5 hours or until the rice and peppers are tender.

Spoon the peppers into dishes and serve with salad and spoonfuls of Greek yogurt flavoured with extra chopped herbs, if liked.

You can vary the herbs used in this recipe, so why not try using chopped basil and chives or rosemary and parsley instead? If you have one or two tomatoes, dice them and then add to the stuffing, too.

Spanish baked potatoes

2 tablespoons olive oil

1 large red onion, thinly sliced

2 garlic cloves, finely chopped

1 teaspoon smoked paprika (pimenton)

1/4–1/2 teaspoon (or to taste) crushed dried red chillies

1 red pepper, cored, deseeded and diced

1 yellow pepper, cored, deseeded and diced

400 g (13 oz) can chopped tomatoes

300 ml (1/2 pint) vegetable stock

2–3 stems of thyme

50 g (2 oz) pitted dry olives

625 g (11/4 lb) baking potatoes, cut into 2.5 cm (1 inch) chunks

salt and pepper

crusty bread, to serve

Preheat the slow cooker if necessary; see the manufacturer's handbook. Heat the oil in a frying pan, add the onion and fry, stirring, for 5 minutes or until just beginning to turn golden.

Stir in the garlic, paprika, dried chillies and peppers and cook for 2 minutes. Mix in the tomatoes, stock, thyme, olives and some salt and pepper, then bring to the boil.

Add the potatoes to the slow cooker pot, pour over the hot tomato mixture, cover with the lid and cook on high for 4–5 hours or until the potatoes are tender. Serve with warm crusty bread.

If you have any leftovers they will taste just as good the next day reheated in the microwave. Try the mixed vegetables topped with a little crumbled feta cheese and a scattering of rocket leaves.

PREPARATION TIME **20 minutes**

COOKING TEMPERATURE **low**

COOKING TIME **6–8 hours**

SERVES **4**

$\mathscr{P}$umpkin &
parmesan gnocchi

1 tablespoon olive oil

25 g (1 oz) butter

1 onion, thinly sliced

2 garlic cloves, finely chopped

2 tablespoons plain flour

150 ml (¼ pint) dry white wine

300 ml (½ pint) vegetable stock

2–3 stems of sage, plus extra to garnish (optional)

400 g (13 oz) pumpkin (or butternut squash), deseeded, peeled, diced and weighed after preparation

500 g (1 lb) chilled gnocchi

125 ml (4 fl oz) double cream

salt and pepper

freshly shaved or grated Parmesan cheese, to garnish

Preheat the slow cooker if necessary; see the manufacturer's handbook. Heat the oil and butter in a frying pan, add the onion and fry, stirring, for 5 minutes or until just beginning to turn golden.

Stir in the garlic, cook for 2 minutes, then stir in the flour. Gradually mix in the wine and stock and heat, stirring until smooth. Add the sage and season well with salt and pepper.

Add the pumpkin to the slow cooker pot, pour over the hot sauce, then press the pumpkin beneath the surface of the liquid. Cover with the lid and cook on low for 6–8 hours or until the pumpkin is tender.

When almost ready to serve, bring a large saucepan of water to the boil, add the gnocchi, bring the water back to the boil and cook for 2–3 minutes or until the gnocchi float to the surface and are piping hot. Tip into a colander to drain.

Stir the cream, then the gnocchi, into the pumpkin, mix together lightly, then spoon into shallow bowls and serve topped with shaved or grated Parmesan and a few extra sage leaves, if liked.

The pumpkin sauce could also be mixed with just-cooked pasta instead of gnocchi and sprinkled with some toasted, roughly chopped hazelnuts or walnuts for a little crunch.

PREPARATION TIME **10 minutes**

COOKING TEMPERATURE **high**

COOKING TIME **4–5 hours**

SERVES **4–6**

Braised celery
with orange

2 celery hearts

grated rind and juice of 1 small
    orange

2 tablespoons light muscovado sugar

400 g (13 oz) can chopped tomatoes

salt and pepper

Preheat the slow cooker if necessary; see the manufacturer's handbook.
Cut each celery heart in half lengthways, then rinse in cold running water
to remove any traces of dirt. Drain and put into the slow cooker pot.

Mix together the remaining ingredients and pour over the celery. Cover
with the lid and cook on high for 4–5 hours or until the celery is tender.

If you would prefer a thicker sauce, pour off the liquid from the slow
cooker pot into a saucepan and boil rapidly for 4–5 minutes to reduce.
Pour back over the celery and serve.

PREPARATION TIME **15 minutes**

COOKING TEMPERATURE **low**

COOKING TIME **6–8 hours**

SERVES **4**

*H*ot pickled beetroot

1 tablespoon olive oil

2 red onions, roughly chopped

1 bunch of beetroot, about 500 g
(1 lb) in total, trimmed, peeled
and cut into 1.5 cm (½ inch)
cubes

1 red-skinned dessert apple, cored
and diced

4 cm (1½ inches) fresh root ginger,
peeled and finely chopped

4 tablespoons red wine vinegar

2 tablespoons clear honey

450 ml (¾ pint) vegetable stock

salt and pepper

TO SERVE

soured cream

dill

Preheat the slow cooker if necessary; see the manufacturer's handbook.
Heat the oil in a frying pan, add the onions and fry, stirring, for
5 minutes or until just beginning to soften and turn golden.

Stir in the beetroot and cook for 3 minutes, then add the apple, ginger,
vinegar and honey. Pour in the stock, add a little salt and pepper and
bring to the boil. Pour the mixture into the slow cooker pot, press the
beetroot below the surface of the liquid, then cover with the lid and
cook on low for 6–8 hours or until tender.

Serve hot as a starter topped with spoonfuls of soured cream and
chopped dill or as a vegetable side dish.

PREPARATION TIME **25 minutes**

COOKING TEMPERATURE **high**

COOKING TIME **1½–2 hours**

SERVES **2**

Aubergine timbale

4 tablespoons olive oil, plus extra
for greasing

1 large aubergine, thinly sliced

1 small onion, chopped

1 garlic clove, finely chopped

½ teaspoon ground cinnamon

¼ teaspoon grated nutmeg

25 g (1 oz) pistachio nuts, roughly
chopped

25 g (1 oz) stoned dates, roughly
chopped

25 g (1 oz) ready-to-eat dried
apricots, roughly chopped

75 g (3 oz) easy-cook white rice

300 ml (½ pint) boiling vegetable
stock

salt and pepper

salad or vine tomatoes, to serve
(optional)

Preheat the slow cooker if necessary; see the manufacturer's handbook.
Lightly oil the base of 2 x 350 ml (12 fl oz) individual soufflé or
straight-sided, heatproof dishes and line the base of each with a circle
of nonstick baking paper, checking first that they will fit into your slow
cooker pot.

Heat 1 tablespoon oil in a frying pan, add one-third of the aubergines
and fry on both sides until softened and golden. Lift out of the pan with
a slotted spoon and transfer to a plate. Repeat with the rest of the
aubergines using 2 more tablespoons of oil.

Heat the remaining 1 tablespoon oil in the pan, add the onion and fry
for 5 minutes or until softened. Stir in the garlic, spices, nuts, fruit and
rice. Season with salt and pepper and mix to combine.

Divide the aubergine slices into 3 piles and arrange one pile in the base
of the 2 dishes, overlapping the slices. Spoon one-quarter of the rice
mixture into each dish, add a second layer of aubergine slices, then
divide the remaining rice equally between the dishes. Top with the
remaining aubergine slices. Pour the stock into the dishes, cover with
lightly oiled foil and put in the slow cooker.

Pour boiling water into the slow cooker to come halfway up the sides
of the dishes. Add the lid and cook on high for 1½–2 hours until the
rice is tender.

Lift the dishes out of the slow cooker with oven gloves. Loosen the
edges of the dishes with a round-bladed knife and turn out the timbales
on to dinner plates. Peel off the lining paper and serve hot with a green
salad or vine tomatoes.

PREPARATION TIME **15 minutes**

COOKING TEMPERATURE **high**

COOKING TIME **3–4 hours**

SERVES **4**

Tarka dhal

250 g (8 oz) red lentils

1 onion, finely chopped

$^{1}/_{2}$ teaspoon turmeric

$^{1}/_{2}$ teaspoon cumin seeds,
    roughly crushed

2 cm ($^{3}/_{4}$ inch) fresh root ginger,
    peeled and finely chopped

200 g (7 oz) canned chopped
    tomatoes

600 ml (1 pint) boiling vegetable
    stock

150 g (5 oz) natural yogurt

salt and pepper

torn coriander leaves,
    to garnish

naan bread, to serve

TARKA

1 tablespoon sunflower oil

2 teaspoons black mustard seeds

$^{1}/_{2}$ teaspoon cumin seeds, roughly
    crushed

pinch of turmeric

2 garlic cloves, finely chopped

Preheat the slow cooker if necessary; see the manufacturer's handbook. Rinse the lentils well with cold water, drain and put in the slow cooker pot with the onion, spices, ginger, tomatoes and boiling stock.

Stir in a little salt and pepper, cover with the lid and cook on high for 3–4 hours or until the lentils are soft and tender.

When almost ready to serve, make the tarka. Heat the oil in a small frying pan, add the mustard and cumin seeds, turmeric and garlic and fry, stirring, for 2 minutes.

Roughly mash the lentil mixture and spoon it into bowls. Add spoonfuls of yogurt and drizzle with the tarka. Garnish with coriander leaves and serve with warm naan bread.

Food for friends

Making supper in the slow cooker takes the effort out of entertaining. You know that your meal is on before your friends arrive and that the food won't spoil if you get a little delayed, so you can relax and enjoy a pre-supper drink.

PREPARATION TIME **15 minutes**

COOKING TEMPERATURE **high**

COOKING TIME **3–4 hours**

SERVES **2–3**

$\mathscr{P}$ot-roast pheasant
with chestnuts

1 pheasant, about 750 g (1½ lb)

25 g (1 oz) butter

1 tablespoon olive oil

200 g (7 oz) shallots, halved

50 g (2 oz) smoked streaky bacon, diced, or ready-diced pancetta

2 celery sticks, thickly sliced

1 tablespoon plain flour

300 ml (½ pint) chicken stock

4 tablespoons dry sherry

100 g (3½ oz) vacuum-packed prepared chestnuts

2–3 sprigs of thyme

salt and pepper

potatoes dauphinois, to serve

Preheat the slow cooker if necessary; see the manufacturer's handbook. Rinse the pheasant inside and out with plenty of cold running water and pat dry with kitchen paper.

Heat the butter and oil in a frying pan, add the pheasant, breast side down, the shallots, bacon or pancetta and celery and fry until golden brown, turning the pheasant and stirring the other ingredients. Transfer the pheasant to the slow cooker pot, placing it breast side down.

Stir the flour into the onion mix. Gradually add the stock and sherry, then add the chestnuts, thyme and a little salt and pepper. Bring to the boil, stirring, then spoon over the pheasant. Cover with the lid and cook on high for 3–4 hours until tender. Test with a knife through the thickest part of the pheasant leg and breast to make sure that the juices run clear.

Carve the pheasant breast into slices and cut the legs away from the body. Serve with potatoes dauphinois.

Chermoula salmon

6 spring onions

25 g (1 oz) parsley

25 g (1 oz) coriander

grated rind and juice of 1 lemon

4 tablespoons olive oil

¹/₂ teaspoon cumin seeds, roughly crushed

500 g (1 lb) thick end salmon fillet, no longer than 18 cm (7 inches), skinned

250 ml (8 fl oz) fish stock

6 tablespoons mayonnaise

125 g (4 oz) mixed salad leaves

salt and pepper

Preheat the slow cooker if necessary; see the manufacturer's handbook. Finely chop the spring onions and herbs with a large knife or in a food processor. Mix with the lemon rind and juice, the oil, cumin seeds and a little salt and pepper.

Rinse the salmon with cold water, drain well and place on a long piece of kitchen foil, the width of the salmon. Press half the herb mixture over both sides of the salmon, then use the foil to lower the fish into the slow cooker pot.

Bring the stock to the boil in a small saucepan, pour over the salmon and tuck the ends of the foil down if needed. Cover with the lid and cook on low for 1³/₄–2¹/₄ hours or until the fish flakes into opaque pieces when pressed in the centre with a knife.

Use the foil to lift the salmon out of the slow cooker pot and transfer to a serving plate. Mix the remaining uncooked herb mixture with the mayonnaise. Arrange the salad leaves on 4 plates. Cut the salmon into 4 pieces and place on the salad. Serve with the herb mayonnaise.

For heartier appetites, toss some thickly sliced, cooked new potatoes with the herb mayonnaise, spoon into the centre of the plates, then top with salad leaves and salmon.

PREPARATION TIME **20 minutes**

COOKING TEMPERATURE **low and high**

COOKING TIME **6¼–8¼ hours**

SERVES **4**

$\mathscr{G}$reen chicken curry

1 tablespoon sunflower oil

2 tablespoons Thai green curry paste

2 teaspoons galangal paste

2 Thai green chillies, deseeded and thinly sliced

1 onion, finely chopped

8 chicken thighs, about 1 kg (2 lb) in total, skinned, boned and cubed

400 ml (14 fl oz) full-fat coconut milk

150 ml (¼ pint) chicken stock

4 dried kaffir lime leaves

2 teaspoons light muscovado sugar

2 teaspoons Thai fish sauce (nam pla)

100 g (3½ oz) sugar snap peas

100 g (3½ oz) green beans, halved

small bunch of coriander, to garnish

rice, to serve

Preheat the slow cooker if necessary; see the manufacturer's handbook. Heat the oil in a frying pan, add the curry paste, galangal paste and green chillies and cook for 1 minute.

Stir in the onion and chicken and cook, stirring, until the chicken is just beginning to turn golden. Pour in the coconut milk and stock, then add the lime leaves, sugar and fish sauce. Bring to the boil, stirring.

Transfer the mixture to the slow cooker pot, cover with the lid and cook on low for 6–8 hours or until the chicken is tender.

Stir in the peas and beans and cook on high for 15 minutes or until they are just tender. Tear the coriander leaves over the top, spoon into bowls and serve with rice.

Thai curry paste and fish sauce are now widely available in all of the larger supermarkets. Galangal paste is sold in small jars and has a gingery taste, while dried kaffir lime leaves can also be found in jars in the same aisle.

$\mathcal{V}$enison puff pie

25 g (1 oz) butter

1 tablespoon olive oil

750 g (1½ lb) diced venison

1 onion, chopped

2 tablespoons plain flour

200 ml (7 fl oz) red wine

250 ml (8 fl oz) lamb or beef stock

3 raw medium beetroot, peeled and
   cut into 1 cm (½ inch) dice

1 tablespoon redcurrant jelly

1 tablespoon tomato purée

10 juniper berries, roughly crushed

3 sprigs of thyme

1 bay leaf

1 sheet, about 200 g (7 oz),
   ready-rolled puff pastry

beaten egg, for glazing

salt and pepper

roasted parsnips and baby carrots,
   to serve

**For a gourmet-style
shepherd's pie the venison
could be topped with creamy
mashed potato flavoured
with garlic, horseradish
and chopped chives.**

Preheat the slow cooker if necessary; see the manufacturer's handbook. Heat the butter and oil in a frying pan, add the venison a few pieces at a time until all the pieces are in the pan, then fry, stirring, until evenly browned. Scoop the venison out of the pan with a slotted spoon and transfer to the slow cooker pot.

Add the onion to the pan juices and fry for 5 minutes until softened. Stir in the flour, then mix in the wine and stock. Add the beetroot, redcurrant jelly and tomato purée, then the juniper, 2 sprigs of thyme and the bay leaf. Season with a little salt and pepper and bring to the boil.

Pour the sauce over the venison, cover with the lid and cook on low for 8–10 hours.

About 30 minutes before you are ready to serve, unroll the pastry, trim the edges to make an oval similar in size to the slow cooker pot. Transfer to a greased baking sheet and flute the edges. Cut leaves from the trimmings and add to pie lid. Brush with egg, sprinkle with the remaining thyme leaves torn from the stem and coarse salt and bake in a preheated oven, 220°C (425°F), Gas 7, for about 20 minutes until well risen and golden.

Stir the venison and spoon on to serving plates. Cut the pastry into portions and place on top of the venison. Serve with roasted parsnips and baby carrots.

Caribbean trout stew

4 small trout, gutted, heads and fins removed and rinsed well with cold water

1 teaspoon ground allspice

1 teaspoon paprika

1 teaspoon ground coriander

2 tablespoons olive oil

6 spring onions, thickly sliced

1 red pepper, cored, deseeded and thinly sliced

2 tomatoes, roughly chopped

½ red hot bonnet or other red chilli, deseeded and chopped

2 sprigs of thyme

300 ml (½ pint) fish stock

salt and pepper

bread, to serve (optional)

Preheat the slow cooker if necessary; see the manufacturer's handbook. Slash the trout on each side 2–3 times with a sharp knife. Mix the spices and a little salt and pepper on a plate and dip each side of the trout in the spice mix.

Heat the oil in a frying pan, add the trout and fry until browned on both sides but not cooked all the way through. Drain and arrange in the slow cooker pot with the fish resting on their lower edges and top to tailing them so that they fit snugly in a single layer.

Add the remaining ingredients to the frying pan with any spices left on the plate and bring to the boil, stirring. Pour over the trout, then cover with the lid and cook on high for 1½–2 hours or until the fish breaks into flakes when pressed in the centre with a knife.

Use a fish slice to lift the fish carefully out of the slow cooker pot and transfer to shallow dishes. Spoon over the sauce and serve with warm bread to mop up the sauce, if liked.

The blend of spices used in this dish is typical of Caribbean fish cookery and although traditionally it would be wrapped in foil and barbecued, it tastes just as good prepared in the slow cooker.

PREPARATION TIME **20 minutes**

COOKING TEMPERATURE **high**

COOKING TIME **5–6 hours**

SERVES **4**

$\mathcal{C}$hinese duck

4 duck legs, each about 200 g (7 oz)

1 onion, sliced

2 tablespoons plain flour

450 ml (¾ pint) chicken stock

2 tablespoons soy sauce

1 tablespoon red wine vinegar

1 tablespoon clear honey

2 teaspoons tomato purée

2 teaspoons Thai fish sauce
    (nam pla)

½ teaspoon crushed dried red chillies

½ teaspoon ground allspice

4 star anise

375 g (12 oz) red plums, stoned and
    quartered

rice or gingered noodles, to serve

Preheat the slow cooker if necessary; see the manufacturer's handbook. Dry-fry the duck legs in a frying pan over a low heat until the fat begins to run, then increase the heat and brown on both sides. Lift them out of the pan with a slotted spoon and transfer to the slow cooker pot.

Pour off all but 1 tablespoon of the duck fat from the pan, then add the onion and fry, stirring, for 5 minutes or until just turning golden. Stir in the flour, then gradually mix in the stock. Add all the remaining ingredients, except the plums, and bring to the boil, stirring.

Pour the sauce over the duck, add the plums and press the duck beneath the surface of the liquid. Cover with the lid and cook on high for 5–6 hours or until the duck is almost falling off the bones. Serve with rice or with gingered noodles.

To make gingered noodles heat 1 tablespoon sesame oil in a wok, add 2.5 cm (1 inch) finely chopped fresh root ginger, 200 g (7 oz) finely shredded pak choi, 50 g (2 oz) halved mangetout and 450 g (14½ oz), straight-to-wok noodles. Stir-fry for 3–4 minutes.

PREPARATION TIME **30 minutes**

COOKING TEMPERATURE **low**

COOKING TIME **1½–2 hours**

SERVES **4**

Salmon-wrapped cod
with buttered leeks

2 cod loins, about 750 g (1½ lb)
   in total

juice of 1 lemon

4 stems of dill, plus extra to garnish
   (optional)

4 slices of smoked salmon, about
   175 g (6 oz) in total

1 leek, thinly sliced; white and green
   parts kept separate

4 tablespoons Noilly Prat or dry
   white wine

200 ml (7 fl oz) boiling fish stock

2 teaspoons drained capers
   (optional)

75 g (3 oz) butter, diced

2 tablespoons chopped chives or
   parsley

salt and pepper

baby new potatoes, to serve
   (optional)

Preheat the slow cooker if necessary; see the manufacturer's handbook. Cut each cod loin in half to give 4 portions, then drizzle with the lemon juice and season with salt and pepper. Add a dill stem to the top of each portion, then wrap with a slice of smoked salmon.

Put the white leek slices into the base of the slow cooker pot, arrange the fish on top in a single layer, tilting them slightly so that they rest slightly at an angle if necessary to make them fit. Add the Noilly Prat and hot stock, then cover and cook on low for 1½–2 hours or until a knife pressed into the centre of one of the fish steaks flakes easily into white pieces.

Carefully lift out the fish with a fish slice and put it on a warm serving plate. Cover with foil and keep hot. Pour the white leeks and cooking juices from the slow cooker into a saucepan, add the green leek slices and the capers (if used) and boil rapidly for about 5 minutes until the liquid is reduced to 4–6 tablespoons. Scoop out and reserve the leeks as soon as the green slices have softened.

Gradually whisk in the butter, a piece at a time until melted, and continue until all the butter has been added and the sauce is smooth and glossy. Return the cooked leeks to the sauce with the chopped herbs and check the seasoning.

Arrange the fish in the centre of 4 serving plates, then spoon the sauce around. Garnish with extra dill and serve with a separate bowl of baby new potatoes, if liked.

PREPARATION TIME **25 minutes**

COOKING TEMPERATURE **high**

COOKING TIME **7–8 hours**

SERVES **4**

$\mathscr{M}$inted lamb
with beetroot couscous

1 tablespoon olive oil

½ shoulder of lamb, 900 g–1 kg
   (1 lb 14 oz–2 lb)

1 onion, sliced

2 garlic cloves, finely chopped

2 tablespoons plain flour

3 tablespoons mint jelly

150 ml (¼ pint) red wine

300 ml (½ pint) lamb stock

salt and pepper

HERBY COUSCOUS

200 g (7 oz) couscous

150 g (5 oz) cooked beetroot, peeled
   and diced

400 ml (14 fl oz) boiling water

grated rind and juice of 1 lemon

2 tablespoons olive oil

small bunch of parsley, finely
   chopped

small bunch of mint, finely chopped

Preheat the slow cooker if necessary; see the manufacturer's handbook. Heat the oil in a frying pan, add the lamb and fry on both sides until browned. Lift out with 2 slotted spoons and transfer to the slow cooker pot. Fry the onion, stirring, for 5 minutes or until softened and just turning golden.

Stir in the garlic, then the flour. Add the mint jelly and wine and mix until smooth. Pour in the stock, season with salt and pepper and bring to the boil, stirring. Pour the sauce over the lamb, cover with the lid and cook on high for 7–8 hours or until the lamb is almost falling off the bone.

When almost ready to serve, put the couscous and beetroot in a bowl, pour over the boiling water, then add the lemon rind and juice, oil and some salt and pepper. Cover with a plate and leave to soak for 5 minutes.

Add the herbs to the couscous and fluff up with a fork, then spoon on to plates. Lift the lamb on to a serving dish and carve into rough pieces, discarding the bone. Arrange on the plates and serve the sauce separately in a jug.

PREPARATION TIME **15 minutes**

COOKING TEMPERATURE **high**

COOKING TIME **3–4 hours**

SERVES **4**

Tarragon chicken

1 tablespoon olive oil

15 g (½ oz) butter

4 boneless, skinless chicken breasts, about 650 g (1 lb 6 oz) in total

200 g (7 oz) shallots, halved

1 tablespoon plain flour

300 ml (½ pint) chicken stock

4 tablespoons dry vermouth

2 sprigs of tarragon, plus extra to serve

3 tablespoons double cream

2 tablespoons chopped chives

salt and pepper

coarsely mashed potatoes mixed with peas, to serve (optional)

Preheat the slow cooker if necessary; see the manufacturer's handbook. Heat the oil and butter in a frying pan, add the chicken and fry over a high heat until golden on both sides but not cooked through. Drain and arrange in the slow cooker pot in a single layer.

Add the shallots to the frying pan and cook, stirring, for 4–5 minutes or until just beginning to turn golden. Stir in the flour, then gradually mix in the stock and vermouth. Add the sprigs of tarragon, a little salt and pepper and bring to the boil, stirring.

Pour the sauce over the chicken, cover with the lid and cook on high for 3–4 hours or until the chicken is cooked through to the centre.

Stir the cream into the sauce and sprinkle over 1 tablespoon chopped tarragon and the chives. Serve with coarsely mashed potatoes mixed with peas.

This is a good basic recipe to adapt to suit what you have in your refrigerator. You could substitute a chopped onion or 4 spring onions for the shallots and sherry or wine for the Vermouth. Try pesto or 1 teaspoon of Dijon mustard instead of the tarragon.

Slow-braised pork
with ratatouille

1 tablespoon olive oil

1 onion, chopped

1 red pepper, cored, deseeded and cut into chunks

1 yellow pepper, cored, deseeded and cut into chunks

375 g (12 oz) courgettes, cut into chunks

2 garlic cloves, finely chopped

400 g (13 oz) can chopped tomatoes

150 ml (¼ pint) red wine or chicken stock

1 tablespoon cornflour

2–3 stems of rosemary, leaves torn from the sprigs

875 g (1¾ lb) piece thick end belly pork, rind and any string removed

salt and pepper

mashed potatoes, to serve

Preheat the slow cooker if necessary; see the manufacturer's handbook. Heat the oil in a frying pan, add the onion and fry, stirring, for 5 minutes or until just beginning to turn golden.

Add the peppers, courgettes and garlic and fry for 2 minutes, then mix in the tomatoes and the wine or stock. Mix the cornflour to a smooth paste with a little water, then stir into the pan with the rosemary leaves and some salt and pepper. Bring to the boil, stirring.

Pour half the mixture into the slow cooker pot, add the unrolled belly pork and cover with the rest of the vegetable mixture. Cover with the lid and cook on high for 7–9 hours or until the pork is almost falling apart.

If you like a thick sauce, ladle the juices out of the slow cooker pot into a saucepan and boil for 5 minutes to reduce. Cut the pork into 4 pieces, then spoon into shallow dishes and serve with mashed potatoes and the tomato sauce.

Belly pork is available in one piece in some supermarkets, but this is a cut that is best bought from your local butcher. Remember to ask for the 'thickest' part of belly pork as this will be leaner and meatier.

$\mathcal{R}$ogan josh

25 g (1 oz) butter

750 g (1½ lb) lamb fillet, sliced

2 onions, chopped

3 garlic cloves, finely chopped

2.5 cm (1 inch) fresh root ginger, peeled and finely chopped

1 teaspoon ground turmeric

2 teaspoons ground coriander

2 teaspoons cumin seeds, roughly crushed

2 teaspoons garam masala

½ teaspoon crushed dried red chillies

2 tablespoons plain flour

400 g (13 oz) can chopped tomatoes

300 ml (½ pint) lamb stock

4 tablespoons double cream

TO GARNISH

small bunch of coriander, leaves torn

red onion, thinly sliced

TO SERVE

pilau rice

naan bread

Preheat the slow cooker if necessary; see the manufacturer's handbook. Heat the butter in a frying pan, add the lamb a few pieces at a time until all the meat is in the pan, then fry, stirring, over a high heat until browned. Lift out of the pan with a slotted spoon and transfer to the slow cooker pot.

Add the onions to the pan and fry, stirring, for 5 minutes or until softened and just beginning to turn golden. Stir in the garlic, ginger, spices and dried chillies and cook for 1 minute. Mix in the flour, then add the tomatoes and stock. Bring to the boil, stirring.

Pour the tomato mixture over the lamb, cover with the lid and cook on low for 8–10 hours or until the lamb is tender. Stir in the cream, garnish with the torn coriander leaves and red onion and serve with pilau rice and naan bread.

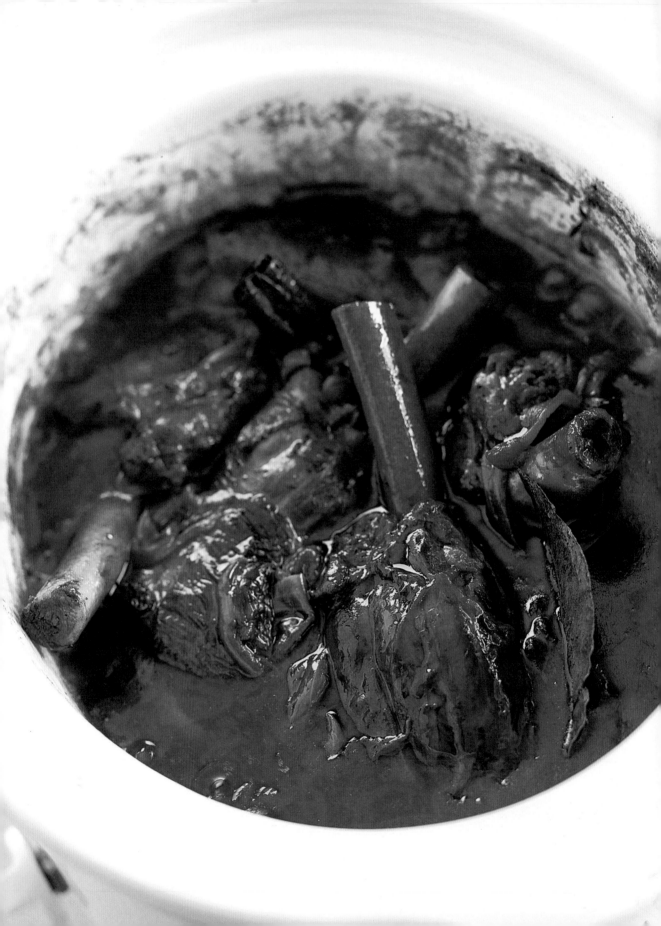

PREPARATION TIME **15 minutes**

COOKING TEMPERATURE **high**

COOKING TIME **5–7 hours**

SERVES **4**

$\mathcal{L}$amb shanks
with juniper

25 g (1 oz) butter

4 lamb shanks, about 1.5 kg (3 lb) in total

2 small red onions, cut into wedges

2 tablespoons plain flour

200 ml (7 fl oz) red wine

450 ml (¾ pint) lamb stock

2 tablespoons cranberry sauce (optional)

1 tablespoon tomato purée

2 bay leaves

1 teaspoon juniper berries, roughly crushed

1 small cinnamon stick, halved

pared rind of 1 small orange

salt and pepper

TO SERVE

mashed sweet potatoes

green beans

Preheat the slow cooker if necessary; see the manufacturer's handbook. Heat the butter in a frying pan, add the lamb shanks and fry over a medium heat, turning until browned all over. Drain and put into the slow cooker pot.

Add the onions to the pan and fry for 4–5 minutes or until just beginning to turn golden. Stir in the flour. Gradually mix in the wine and stock, then add the cranberry sauce (if used) and the remaining ingredients. Bring to the boil, stirring.

Transfer the mixture to the slow cooker pot, cover with the lid and cook on high for 5–7 hours or until the lamb is beginning to fall off the bone. If you like thick sauces, pour the sauce into a pan and boil rapidly for 5 minutes or until reduced by one-third. Serve the lamb with mashed sweet potatoes and green beans.

Puddings

The slow cooker is perfect for getting organized. You can bake and chill a custard-style dessert or fruit compote or put on a hot pudding well in advance and then relax. It won't matter if the main course takes longer than you'd planned – just dish up when you're ready.

PREPARATION TIME **20 minutes**

COOKING TEMPERATURE **low**

COOKING TIME **3–4 hours**

SERVES **4**

*S*affron pears
with chocolate

300 ml (½ pint) cloudy apple juice

3 tablespoons caster sugar

large pinch of saffron threads

4 cardamom pods, roughly crushed

4 firm, ripe pears

CHOCOLATE SAUCE

4 tablespoons chocolate and hazelnut
    spread

2 tablespoons double cream

2 tablespoons milk

Preheat the slow cooker if necessary; see the manufacturer's handbook. Pour the apple juice into a small saucepan, add the sugar, saffron and cardamom pods and their tiny black seeds. Bring to the boil, then tip into the slow cooker pot.

Cut each pear in half lengthways, leaving the stalk on, then cut away the skin. Remove the pear cores with a melon baller, if you have one, or a teaspoon. Add the pears to the slow cooker pot, pressing them beneath the surface of the liquid as much as you can. Cover with the lid and cook on low for 3–4 hours or until the pears are tender and pale yellow.

When you are almost ready to serve, put all the ingredients for the sauce into a small saucepan and warm together, stirring until smooth. Spoon the pears and some of the saffron sauce into shallow dishes, then pour the chocolate sauce into a small jug to allow your guests to drizzle the sauce over the pears just before eating.

PREPARATION TIME **20 minutes**

COOKING TEMPERATURE **high**

COOKING TIME **1¼–1½ hours**

SERVES **4**

Chocolate puddings

125 g (4 oz) plain dark chocolate,
plus 8 extra small squares

75 g (3 oz) butter

2 eggs

2 egg yolks

75 g (3 oz) caster sugar

½ teaspoon vanilla extract

40 g (1½ oz) plain flour

sifted icing sugar, to decorate

TO SERVE

mini marshmallows

vanilla ice cream or crème fraîche

Preheat the slow cooker if necessary; see the manufacturer's handbook. Break the 125 g (4 oz) chocolate into pieces, put them into a saucepan with the butter and heat gently, stirring occasionally, until melted. Take off the heat and set aside.

Whisk together the whole eggs, egg yolks, sugar and vanilla extract in a large bowl with an electric whisk for 3–4 minutes or until light and frothy. Gradually whisk in the melted chocolate mixture.

Sift the flour into the chocolate mix and fold together. Pour into 4 x 250 ml (8 fl oz) buttered and base-lined individual metal pudding moulds. Press 2 squares of chocolate into the centre of each one, then loosely cover the tops with squares of buttered foil.

Transfer the pudding moulds to the slow cooker pot and pour boiling water into the pot to come halfway up the sides of the moulds. Cover with the lid and cook on high for 1¼–1½ hours until well risen and the pudding tops spring back when lightly pressed.

Loosen the puddings with a knife, turn out into shallow serving dishes and remove the lining paper. Sprinkle with sifted icing sugar and serve with marshmallows and spoonfuls of vanilla ice cream or crème fraîche.

Crème caramels

butter, for greasing

125 g (4 oz) granulated sugar

125 ml (4 fl oz) water

2 tablespoons boiling water

2 eggs

3 egg yolks

400 g (13 oz) can full-fat condensed milk

125 ml (4 fl oz) semi-skimmed milk

grated rind of ½ small lemon

Preheat the slow cooker if necessary; see the manufacturer's handbook. Lightly butter 4 x 250 ml (8 fl oz) individual metal pudding moulds. Pour the sugar and water into a small saucepan and heat gently, stirring occasionally until the sugar has completely dissolved.

Increase the heat and boil the syrup for 5 minutes, without stirring, until it has turned golden, keeping a watchful eye as it cooks. Take the pan off the heat, add the boiling water and stand well back.

Tilt the pan to mix, and when the bubbles have subsided pour the caramel sauce into the pudding moulds, tilting them so that the syrup coats the base and sides.

Put the eggs and egg yolks into a bowl and fork together. Pour the condensed milk and fresh milk into a saucepan, bring to the boil, then gradually beat into the egg mixture until smooth. Strain back into the pan, then stir in the lemon rind.

Pour the custard into the syrup-lined pudding moulds, then transfer the moulds to the slow cooker pot. Cover the top of each mould with a square of foil. Pour hot water around the moulds so that the water comes halfway up the sides, then cover with the lid and cook on low for 2½–3½ hours or until the custard is set with just a slight wobble in the centre.

If you haven't made caramel sauce before resist the urge to stir it once it is boiling or you may find that the sauce crystalizes before it has a chance to brown.

Lift the moulds out of the slow cooker pot with a tea towel, allow to cool then transfer to the refrigerator for 3–4 hours or overnight to chill.

To serve, dip the base of the moulds into boiling water for 10 seconds, loosen the top of the custard with a fingertip, then turn out on to rimmed plates.

PREPARATION TIME **30 minutes, plus chilling**

COOKING TEMPERATURE **high**

COOKING TIME **2–2½ hours**

SERVES **4–5**

$\mathscr{S}$trawberry cheesecake

4 trifle sponges

300 g (10 oz) full-fat cream cheese

75 g (3 oz) caster sugar

150 ml (¼ pint) double cream

3 eggs

grated rind and juice of ½ lemon

TOPPING

2 tablespoons strawberry jam

1 tablespoon lemon juice

200 g (7 oz) strawberries, hulled
   and sliced

Preheat the slow cooker if necessary; see the manufacturer's handbook. Use nonstick baking paper to line the base and sides of a soufflé dish that is 14 cm (5½ inches) in diameter and 9 cm (3½ inches) high. Line the base with the trifle sponges, trimming them to fit in an even layer.

Put the cream cheese and sugar in a bowl, then gradually whisk in the cream until smooth and thick. Gradually whisk in the eggs one at a time, then mix in the lemon rind and juice.

Pour the cream cheese mixture into the prepared dish and spread level. Cover the top of the dish loosely with buttered foil and lower it into the slow cooker pot with foil straps (see page 17). Pour boiling water into the pot to come halfway up the sides of the dish.

Cover with the lid and cook on high for 2–2½ hours until the cheesecake is puffy and well risen and softly set in the middle. Take the dish out of the slow cooker and leave to cool and firm up. The cheesecake will sink quickly as it cools to about the size that it was before cooking. When it is cool, transfer to the refrigerator for 4 hours or overnight.

When ready to serve, loosen the edges of the cheesecake with a round-bladed knife, turn it out, peel off the paper and turn it the right way up. Put it on a serving plate. Mix the jam and lemon juice in a bowl until smooth, add the sliced strawberries and toss together. Spoon on top of the cheesecake and serve immediately.

Choose whatever fruits are in season. We used sliced strawberries, but you could use mixed berry fruits or diced peaches and raspberries if you prefer.

PREPARATION TIME **10 minutes**

COOKING TEMPERATURE **low**

COOKING TIME **2½–3 hours**

SERVES **4**

ℋoneyed rice pudding

butter for greasing

750 ml (1¼ pints) full-fat Jersey milk

3 tablespoons set honey

125 g (4 oz) risotto rice

TO SERVE

jam

thick cream

Preheat the slow cooker if necessary; see the manufacturer's handbook. Lightly butter the inside of the slow cooker pot.

Pour the milk into a saucepan, add the honey and bring just to the boil, stirring until the honey has melted. Pour into the slow cooker pot, add the rice and stir gently.

Cover with the lid and cook on low for 2½–3 hours, stirring once during cooking, or until the pudding is thickened and the rice is soft. Stir again just before spooning into dishes and serve topped with spoonfuls of jam (or the apricot conserve on page 224) and thick cream.

$\mathcal{B}$aked apples
with dates

50 g (2 oz) butter at room
temperature

50 g (2 oz) light muscovado sugar

1/2 teaspoon ground cinnamon

grated rind of 1/2 small orange

1 tablespoon finely chopped glacé or
drained stem ginger

50 g (2 oz) ready-chopped stoned
dates

4 large, firm dessert apples, such as
Braeburn

150 ml (1/4 pint) cloudy apple juice

custard or cream, to serve

Preheat the slow cooker if necessary; see the manufacturer's handbook.
Mix together the butter, sugar, cinnamon and orange rind until smooth,
then stir in the chopped ginger and dates.

Trim a thin slice off the bottom of the apples, if needed, so that they will
stand up without rolling over, then cut a thick slice off the top of each
and reserve for later. Using a small knife, cut away the apple core to
leave a cavity for the stuffing.

Divide the date mixture into 4 and press a portion into each apple cavity,
spreading it over the top cut edge of the apple if it won't all fit in.
Replace the apple lids and put the apples into the slow cooker pot. Pour
the apple juice into the base of the pot, cover with the lid and cook on
low for 3–4 hours or until the apples are tender.

Lift the apples carefully out of the slow cooker and serve in shallow
dishes with the sauce spooned over and a drizzle of hot custard
or cream.

PREPARATION TIME **20 minutes**

COOKING TEMPERATURE **high**

COOKING TIME **3–3½ hours**

SERVES **4–5**

*S*ticky marmalade
syrup pudding

4 tablespoons golden syrup

3 tablespoons orange marmalade

175 g (6 oz) self-raising flour

75 g (3 oz) shredded vegetable suet

50 g (2 oz) light muscovado sugar

1 teaspoon ground ginger

grated rind and juice of 1 orange

2 eggs

2 tablespoons milk

custard or vanilla ice cream, to serve

Preheat the slow cooker if necessary; see the manufacturer's handbook. Lightly butter a 1.2 litre (2 pint) pudding basin (checking first that it will fit into your slow cooker pot) and line the base with a circle of nonstick baking paper. Spoon the golden syrup and 2 tablespoons of the marmalade into the pot.

Put the flour, suet, sugar and ginger in a bowl and mix together. Add the remaining marmalade, orange rind and juice, the eggs and milk and beat until smooth.

Spoon the mixture into the pudding basin, level the surface and cover the top of the basin with a piece of buttered foil. Lower into the slow cooker pot, using foil straps or string (see page 17). Pour boiling water into the pot to come halfway up the sides of the basin.

Cover with the lid and cook on high for 3–3½ hours or until the pudding is well risen and feels firm and dry when the top is pressed with a fingertip.

Lift the basin out of the slow cooker with oven gloves, remove the foil and loosen the edge of the pudding with a round-bladed knife. Invert the basin on a plate, remove the basin and peel off the lining paper. Serve scoops of the pudding with custard or vanilla ice cream.

This pudding is delicious served drizzled with fresh or canned custard, especially if it's flavoured with a few tablespoons of sherry, Grand Marnier or Cointreau.

PREPARATION TIME **25 minutes**

COOKING TEMPERATURE **high**

COOKING TIME **4¹/₂–5 hours**

SERVES **6**

$\mathcal{I}$ced Jamaican
ginger cake

100 g (3¹/₂ oz) butter, plus extra for greasing

100 g (3¹/₂ oz) dark muscovado sugar

100 g (3¹/₂ oz) golden syrup

100 g (3¹/₂ oz) ready-chopped stoned dates

100 g (3¹/₂ oz) wholemeal plain flour

100 g (3¹/₂ oz) self-raising flour

¹/₂ teaspoon bicarbonate of soda

2 teaspoons ground ginger

3 pieces of stem ginger, drained , 2 chopped and 1 cut into strips

2 eggs, beaten

100 ml (3¹/₂ fl oz) milk

125 g (4 oz) icing sugar, sifted

3–3¹/₂ teaspoons water

Preheat the slow cooker if necessary; see the manufacturer's handbook. Butter a soufflé dish that is 14 cm (5¹/₂ inches) in diameter and 9 cm (3¹/₂ inches) high and base-line with a circle of nonstick baking paper.

Put the measured butter, sugar, syrup and dates into a saucepan and heat gently, stirring, until the butter and sugar have melted. Take the pan off the heat, add the flours, bicarbonate of soda, ground and chopped ginger, eggs and milk and beat until smooth. Pour into the lined dish and cover the top loosely with buttered foil.

Lower the dish carefully into the slow cooker pot on foil straps (see page 17) or tie string around the top edge of the dish. Pour boiling water into the pot to come halfway up the sides of the dish, cover with the lid and cook on high for 4¹/₂–5 hours or until a skewer comes out cleanly when inserted into the centre of the ginger cake.

Take the dish out of the slow cooker pot, leave to stand for 10 minutes, then remove the foil and loosen the edge of the cake with a round-bladed knife. Turn out the cake on a wire rack, peel off the lining paper and leave to cool.

Sift the icing sugar into a bowl and mix in just enough water to make a smooth, thick icing. Spoon over the top of the cake, then decorate with the strips of ginger. Leave to set. Cut the cake into wedges to serve.

PREPARATION TIME **30 minutes, plus chilling**

COOKING TEMPERATURE **low**

COOKING TIME **2½–3½ hours**

SERVES **4**

Peppermint
& raspberry brûlée

4 egg yolks

40 g (1½ oz) caster sugar

400 ml (14 fl oz) double cream

¼ teaspoon peppermint essence

150 g (5 oz) raspberries

2 tablespoons icing sugar

mint leaves, to decorate (optional)

Preheat the slow cooker if necessary; see the manufacturer's handbook. Whisk the egg yolks and sugar in a bowl for 3–4 minutes until frothy, then gradually whisk in the cream.

Stir in the peppermint essence then strain the egg custard into a jug. Pour into 4 x 150 ml (¼ pint) ramekin dishes.

Put the dishes into the slow cooker pot, pour hot water into the pot to come halfway up the sides of the dishes, then loosely cover the top of each dish with foil. Cook on low for 2½–3½ hours or until the custard is set with a slight quiver to the centre.

Carefully lift the dishes out of the slow cooker, allow to cool then transfer to the refrigerator for 4 hours to chill.

When ready to serve, pile a few raspberries in the centre of each dish and sprinkle over some icing sugar. Caramelize the sugar with a cook's blow torch and decorate with a few tiny mint leaves, if liked.

If you don't have a cook's blow torch, pop the ramekins under a preheated hot grill instead. Omit the raspberries, sprinkle the dishes with sugar and put in a roasting tin with ice so that the custards stay cold as the sugar topping melts and caramelizes.

PREPARATION TIME **20 minutes**

COOKING TEMPERATURE **high**

COOKING TIME **2–2½ hours**

SERVES **4**

$\mathscr{P}$ineapple
upside-down puddings

butter, for greasing

4 tablespoons golden syrup

2 tablespoons light muscovado sugar

225 g (7½ oz) can pineapple rings, drained and chopped

40 g (1½ oz) glacé cherries, roughly chopped

custard, to serve (optional)

SPONGE

50 g (2 oz) butter at room temperature or soft margarine

50 g (2 oz) caster sugar

50 g (2 oz) self-raising flour

25 g (1 oz) desiccated coconut

1 egg

1 tablespoon milk

Preheat the slow cooker if necessary; see the manufacturer's handbook. Lightly butter 4 x 250 ml (8 fl oz) individual metal pudding moulds and base-line with a circle of nonstick baking paper. Add 1 tablespoon golden syrup and ½ tablespoon sugar to the base of each, then add three-quarters of the pineapple and all the cherries.

Make the sponge. Put all the ingredients for the sponge and the remaining pineapple into a bowl and beat together until smooth. Spoon the mixture into the pudding moulds. Level the surface with the back of a small spoon, then cover the top of each mould loosely with buttered foil.

Stand the moulds in the slow cooker pot, then pour boiling water into the pot to come halfway up the sides of the moulds. Cover with the lid and cook on high for 2–2½ hours or until the sponge is well risen and springs back when pressed with a fingertip.

Remove the foil, loosen the edges of the puddings with a round-bladed knife and turn out into shallow bowls. Peel away the lining paper and serve with hot custard, if liked.

Add a couple of tablespoons of your favourite canned fruit pie filling to the base of the moulds, adding a little grated orange rind to sponge instead of the pineapple.

$\mathcal{H}$ot toddy oranges

8 clementines

50 g (2 oz) honey

75 g (3 oz) soft light muscovado
sugar

grated rind and juice of ½ lemon

4 tablespoons whisky

300 ml (½ pint) boiling water

15 g (½ oz) butter

ice cream, to serve

Preheat the slow cooker if necessary; see the manufacturer's handbook. Peel the clementines but leave them whole.

Place the remaining ingredients in the slow cooker pot and mix together. Add the oranges. Cover with the lid and cook on low for 2–3 hours until piping hot.

Spoon into shallow dishes and serve with just-melting scoops of vanilla ice cream.

This warming winter pudding can also be made with 4 large oranges instead of clementines. Peel and cut them into horizontal slices or divide into segments, if preferred.

$\mathscr{L}$emon & poppy seed
drizzle cake

125 g (4 oz) butter at room
  temperature, plus extra
  for greasing

125 g (4 oz) caster sugar

2 eggs, beaten

125 g (4 oz) self-raising flour

2 tablespoons poppy seeds

grated rind of 1 lemon

crème fraîche, to serve

lemon rind curls, to decorate

LEMON SYRUP

juice of 1¹/₂ lemons

125 g (4 oz) caster sugar

Preheat the slow cooker if necessary; see the manufacturer's handbook. Lightly butter a soufflé dish that is 14 cm (5¹/₂ inches) in diameter and 9 cm (3¹/₂ inches) high, and base-line it with a circle of nonstick baking paper.

Cream together the measured butter and sugar in a bowl with a wooden spoon or electric hand mixer. Gradually mix in alternate spoonfuls of beaten egg and flour and continue adding and beating until the mixture is smooth. Stir in the poppy seeds and lemon rind, then spoon the mixture into the soufflé dish and level the top. Cover the top of the dish loosely with buttered foil and then lower into the slow cooker pot using foil straps (see page 17).

Pour boiling water into the slow cooker pot so that it comes halfway up the sides of the dish. Cover with the lid and cook on high for 4¹/₂–5 hours or until the cake is dry and springs back when pressed with a fingertip.

Lift the dish carefully out of the slow cooker with a tea towel, remove the foil and loosen the edge of the cake with a round-bladed knife. Turn out on to a plate or shallow dish with a rim and remove the lining paper.

Quickly warm together the lemon juice and sugar for the syrup and pour the syrup over the cake as soon as the sugar has dissolved. Leave to cool and for the syrup to soak in. Cut into slices and serve with spoonfuls of crème fraîche, decorated with lemon rind curls.

PREPARATION TIME **20 minutes**

COOKING TEMPERATURE **high**

COOKING TIME **7–8 hours**

REHEATING TIME **2–2$\frac{1}{2}$ hours**

SERVES **6–8**

Christmas pudding

butter, for greasing

750 g (1$\frac{1}{2}$ lb) mixed luxury dried
fruit, larger fruits diced

50 g (2 oz) pistachio nuts, roughly
chopped

25 g (1 oz) glacé or stem ginger,
finely chopped

1 dessert apple, peeled, cored and
coarsely grated

grated rind and juice of 1 lemon

grated rind and juice of 1 orange

4 tablespoons brandy

50 g (2 oz) soft dark muscovado
sugar

50 g (2 oz) self-raising flour

75 g (3 oz) breadcrumbs

100 g (3$\frac{1}{2}$ oz) vegetable suet

1 teaspoon ground mixed spice

2 eggs, beaten

TO SERVE

4 tablespoons brandy (optional)

brandy butter or cream

Preheat the slow cooker if necessary; see the manufacturer's handbook. Check that a 1.5 litre (2$\frac{1}{2}$ pint) pudding basin will fit inside your slow cooker pot with a little room to spare, then butter the inside of the basin and base-line with a circle of nonstick baking paper.

Put the dried fruit, nuts, ginger and grated apple into a large bowl. Add the fruit rinds and juice and brandy and mix together well. Stir in the remaining ingredients. Spoon into the buttered basin, pressing down well as you go. Cover with a large circle of nonstick baking paper, then a piece of foil. Tie with string and add a string handle.

Lower into the slow cooker pot, using string handles (see page 17) and pour boiling water into the pot to come two-thirds up the sides of the basin. Cover with the lid and cook on high for 7–8 hours. Check halfway through cooking and top up with extra boiling water if needed. Take the pudding out of the slow cooker with a tea towel and leave to cool.

Cover the pudding with fresh foil, leaving the baking paper in place. Fasten with string and keep in a cool place for 2 months or until Christmas.

To serve, preheat the slow cooker if necessary, add the pudding and boiling water as above and reheat on high for 2–2$\frac{1}{2}$ hours. Remove the foil and paper, loosen the pudding and turn it out. Warm the brandy (if used) in a saucepan. When it is just boiling, flame with a taper and quickly pour over the pudding. Serve with brandy butter or cream.

*W*inter berry compote

300 g (10 oz) cranberries

500 g (1 lb) red plums, quartered and stoned

200 g (7 oz) red seedless grapes, halved

4 teaspoons cornflour

300 ml (½ pint) red grape juice

100 g (3½ oz) caster sugar

1 cinnamon stick, halved

pared rind of 1 small orange

LEMON CURD CREAM

150 ml (¼ pint) double cream, lightly whipped

3 tablespoons lemon curd

Preheat the slow cooker if necessary; see the manufacturer's handbook. Put the cranberries, plums and grapes into the slow cooker pot.

Mix the cornflour with a little of the grape juice in a bowl until smooth, then stir in the remaining juice. Pour into the slow cooker pot and add the sugar, cinnamon and orange rind. Stir together, then cover with the lid and cook on low for 2½–3½ hours or until the fruit is tender.

Stir the compote, discard the cinnamon and serve warm or cold spooned into bowls and topped with the Lemon Curd Cream, if liked.

PREPARATION TIME **10 minutes**

COOKING TEMPERATURE **low**

COOKING TIME **1½–2 hours**

SERVES **4**

*S*ticky rum bananas
with vanilla

25 g (1 oz) butter

75 g (3 oz) light muscovado sugar

grated rind and juice of 1 lime

1 vanilla pod or 1 teaspoon vanilla
extract

3 tablespoons white or dark rum

200 ml (7 fl oz) boiling water

6 small bananas, peeled and halved
lengthways

curls of lime rind, to decorate

vanilla ice cream, to serve (optional)

Preheat the slow cooker if necessary; see the manufacturer's handbook.
Add the butter, sugar and lime rind and juice to the slow cooker pot as it
is warming up and stir until the butter has melted.

Slit the vanilla pod along its length, open it out with a small, sharp knife
and scrape the tiny black seeds away from inside the pod. Add the seeds
and the pod or vanilla extract (if used) to the slow cooker pot along with
the rum and boiling water.

Add the bananas to the slow cooker pot, arranging them in a single layer
and pressing them beneath the liquid as much as you can. Cover with
the lid and cook on low for 1½–2 hours or until the bananas are hot.

Spoon the bananas and rum sauce into dishes and decorate with extra
lime rind curls and scoops of vanilla ice cream, if liked.

Drinks & preserves

Warming party mulled wines and punches are easy to make in a slow cooker. You can also make gourmet-style fruit conserves, marmalades, jellies and savoury chutneys, which make unusual and welcome gifts.

$\mathcal{B}$eetroot chutney

1 bunch of raw beetroot, about 5 beetroot, trimmed and peeled

500 g (1 lb) red plums, stoned and roughly chopped

1 large onion, finely chopped

250 ml (8 fl oz) red wine vinegar

250 g (8 oz) soft light muscovado sugar

4 cm (1½ inch) fresh root ginger, peeled and finely chopped

1 tablespoon star anise pieces, crushed using a pestle and mortar

1 teaspoon peppercorns, crushed using a pestle and mortar

1 teaspoon ground cinnamon

Preheat the slow cooker if necessary; see the manufacturer's handbook. Coarsely grate the beetroot and put it into the slow cooker pot with all the remaining ingredients.

Mix everything together thoroughly, then cover with the lid and cook on high for 6–7 hours, stirring once or twice, until the beetroot is tender and the plums pulpy.

Stand 4 clean jam jars in a roasting tin and warm in a low oven for 5 minutes until hot. Ladle the hot chutney into the jars, smooth the surface flat with a teaspoon, cover with waxed discs and screw the lids in place. Label and store in a cool place until required. Once opened, store in the refrigerator. Serve with cheese, cold sliced ham or with the Courgette & Broad Bean Frittata (see pages 48–49).

Wear rubber gloves while you're peeling the beetroot so that your hands don't get stained, and grate the beetroot in a food processor fitted with a coarse grater blade.

PREPARATION TIME **40 minutes**

COOKING TEMPERATURE **high**

COOKING TIME **2–3 hours**

MAKES **3 jars**

$\mathscr{A}$pple, thyme &
rosemary jelly

1 kg (2 lb) cooking apples (not peeled or cored), washed and diced

125 ml (4 fl oz) red wine or cider vinegar

600 ml (1 pint) boiling water

about 625 g (1¼ lb) granulated sugar

1 tablespoon thyme leaves, stripped from the stems

2 tablespoons finely chopped rosemary leaves

Preheat the slow cooker if necessary; see the manufacturer's handbook. Put the apples and vinegar into the slow cooker pot and pour over the boiling water.

Cover with the lid and cook on high for 2–3 hours until the apples are soft. Don't worry if the apples discolour slightly while cooking; this will not affect the finished jelly.

Hang a jelly bag from a frame or upturned stool and set a bowl beneath it. Ladle the cooked apple and juices into the bag and allow to drip through. Don't be tempted to press the liquid through the bag with a spoon or the finished jelly will be cloudy.

Measure the liquid and pour it into a large saucepan; for every 600 ml (1 pint) liquid add 500 g (1 lb) of sugar. Heat gently, stirring occasionally, until the sugar has dissolved, then boil rapidly for about 15 minutes until setting point is reached. Check with a jam thermometer or spoon a little of the jelly on to a saucer that has been chilled in the refrigerator. Leave for 1–2 minutes then run a finger through the jelly. If a finger space is left and the jelly has wrinkled it is ready; if not boil for 5–10 minutes more and then retest.

Skim any scum with a slotted spoon, then stir in the chopped herbs. Leave the jelly to stand for 5 minutes so that the herbs don't float to the surface, then ladle it into warm, dry jars. Add a waxed disc to each, cover with a cellophane jam pot cover and secure with an elastic band. Label and store in a cool place until required. Once opened, store the jelly in the refrigerator. Serve as an accompaniment to roast lamb.

If you don't have a jelly bag, improvise with a large sieve set over a saucepan and line it a with new fabric dishcloth that has been rinsed with boiling water.

PREPARATION TIME **45 minutes, plus cooling**

COOKING TEMPERATURE **low**

COOKING TIME **8–10 hours**

MAKES **6 jars of assorted sizes**

*O*range marmalade

1 kg (2 lb) Seville oranges

1.2 litre (2 pints) boiling water

2 kg (4 lb) preserving or
   granulated sugar

Preheat the slow cooker if necessary; see the manufacturer's handbook. Put the whole oranges into the slow cooker pot, cover with the boiling water and put an upturned saucer on top of the oranges to stop them from floating.

Cover with the lid and cook on low for 8–10 hours until the oranges are tender. Leave to cool in the slow cooker overnight.

The next day lift the oranges out of the slow cooker, draining well. Cut in quarters, scoop out and discard the pips, then thinly slice the oranges.

Put the sliced oranges and the liquid from the slow cooker pot into a preserving pan or large saucepan, add the sugar and heat gently, stirring occasionally until the sugar has completely dissolved.

Increase the heat, add a sugar thermometer if you have one and boil for 20–30 minutes or until setting point is reached (see page 220 for how to test). Meanwhile, warm 6 jars in a warm oven.

Ladle the hot marmalade into the warm jars, cover the surface with waxed discs, add cellophane jam tops and secure with elastic bands or screw the jar lids in place. Label and store in a cool place until required.

Seville oranges are in season for only 6 weeks or so. To make a similar marmalade out of season use small oranges and add the juice of 1 lemon together with the sugar.

*A*pricot conserve

300 g (10 oz) ready-to-eat dried
    apricots, diced

4 peaches, halved, stoned and diced

250 g (8 oz) caster sugar

300 ml (½ pint) boiling water

Preheat the slow cooker if necessary; see the manufacturer's handbook. Put the apricots, peaches, sugar and boiling water into the slow cooker pot and stir together.

Cover with the lid and cook on high for 3–5 hours, stirring once during cooking and then again at the end. Cook until the fruit is soft and the liquid thick and syrupy, with a texture like chutney.

Ladle the conserve into warm jars. Cover the surface with waxed discs, then a cellophane jam pot cover and fasten with an elastic band. Leave to cool. The conserve can be stored for up to 2 months in the refrigerator.

If you would prefer to peel the peaches, cut a cross in the base of each one and plunge into boiling water for 1 minute. The skin will easily peel away.

PREPARATION TIME **15 minutes**

COOKING TEMPERATURE **low**

COOKING TIME **3–4 hours**

MAKES **3 small jars**

*P*assion fruit
& lime curd

125 g (4 oz) unsalted butter, diced

400 g (13 oz) caster sugar

4 eggs, beaten

grated rind and juice of 2 limes

grated rind of 2 lemons

juice of 1 lemon

3 passion fruit, halved

Preheat the slow cooker if necessary; see the manufacturer's handbook. Put the butter and sugar in a large basin (double-check that it will fit into the slow cooker before you continue), then microwave for 2 minutes on full power until the butter has just melted.

Stir the sugar mix, then gradually whisk in the eggs, and then the fruit rind and juice. Cover the basin with foil and put it into the slow cooker pot. Pour boiling water into the pot to come halfway up the sides of the basin, cover with the lid and cook on low for 3–4 hours, stirring once during cooking, until thick.

Stir the preserve once more. Scoop the passion fruit seeds out of the halved fruit with a teaspoon and stir them into the preserve.

Ladle the preserve into warmed jars, cover the surface with waxed discs, then a cellophane jam pot cover and fasten with an elastic band. Leave to cool. The preserve can be stored for up to 2 weeks in the refrigerator.

PREPARATION TIME **10 minutes**

COOKING TEMPERATURE **high and low**

COOKING TIME **3–4 hours**

SERVES **6**

$\mathcal{C}$ider toddy

1 litre (1¾ pints) dry cider

125 ml (4 fl oz) whisky

125 ml (4 fl oz) orange juice

4 tablespoons set honey

2 cinnamon sticks, halved

1 orange, cut into wedges and
  orange rind curls, to decorate
  (optional)

Preheat the slow cooker if necessary; see the manufacturer's handbook. Add all the ingredients to the slow cooker pot, cover with the lid and cook on high for 1 hour.

Reduce the heat and cook on low for 2–3 hours until piping hot. Stir, then ladle into heatproof tumblers. Add orange wedges and curls to decorate, if liked.

$\mathcal{M}$ulled wine

750 ml (1¼ pints) or 1 bottle
   inexpensive red wine

300 ml (½ pint) clear apple juice

300 ml (½ pint) water

juice of 1 orange

1 orange, sliced

½ lemon, sliced

1 cinnamon stick, halved

6 cloves

2 bay leaves

Preheat the slow cooker if necessary; see the manufacturer's handbook. Pour the wine, apple juice, water and orange juice into the slow cooker pot. Add the sliced orange and lemon, the cinnamon stick, cloves and bay leaves, then mix in the sugar and brandy.

Cover with the lid and cook on high for 1 hour. Reduce to low and cook for 3–4 hours.

PREPARATION TIME **10 minutes**

COOKING TEMPERATURE **high and low**

COOKING TIME **3–4 hours**

SERVES **6**

$\mathcal{H}$ot spiced berry punch

1 litre (1¾ pints) cranberry and
  raspberry drink

250 g (8 oz) frozen berry fruits

50 g (2 oz) caster sugar

4 tablespoons crème de cassis
  (optional)

4 small star anise

1 cinnamon stick, halved lengthways

fresh raspberries, to decorate
  (optional)

Preheat the slow cooker if necessary; see the manufacturer's handbook.
Pour the cranberry and raspberry drink into the slow cooker pot, add
the frozen fruits, the sugar and crème de cassis (if used). Stir together,
then add the star anise and halved cinnamon stick. Cover with the lid
and cook on high for 1 hour.

Reduce the heat to low and cook for 2–3 hours. Strain if liked, then
take out the star anise and cinnamon and add these to serving tumblers.
Pour the hot punch into small heatproof glasses and add a few fresh
raspberries, if liked.

**This is an adaptable drink for parties. For a
non-alcoholic, driver-friendly version, omit
the cassis. You can also omit the cassis and
purée the drink until smooth for a warming
toddy for children or you could make a
cider-, fruit juice- or tea-based punch instead.**

PREPARATION TIME **5 minutes**

COOKING TEMPERATURE **high and low**

COOKING TIME **3–4 hours**

SERVES **6**

$\mathcal{H}$ot buttered rum

1 litre (1¾ pints) clear apple juice

150 ml (¼ pint) dark rum

2 tablespoons set honey

2 tablespoons dark muscovado sugar

25 g (1 oz) butter

6 cloves

1 dessert apple, cored and
thickly sliced, to decorate

Preheat the slow cooker if necessary; see the manufacturer's handbook. Pour the apple juice, rum, honey, sugar, butter and cloves into the slow cooker pot.

Cover with the lid and cook on high for 1 hour. Reduce the heat and cook on low for 3–4 hours. Stir, scoop out the cloves then ladle the punch into heatproof tumblers. Decorate with slices of apple.

PREPARATION TIME **10 minutes**

COOKING TEMPERATURE **low**

COOKING TIME **2–3 hours**

SERVES **4**

$\mathscr{S}$kier's hot chocolate

100 g (3½ oz) good quality
   chocolate

25 g (1 oz) caster sugar

750 ml (1¼ pints) full-fat milk

few drops of vanilla extract

little ground cinnamon

3 tablespoons kahlua coffee liqueur
   (optional)

mini marshmallows, to serve

Preheat the slow cooker if necessary; see the manufacturer's handbook. Place the chocolate and sugar in the slow cooker pot, then add the milk, vanilla extract and cinnamon.

Cover with the lid and cook on low for 2–3 hours, whisking once or twice, until the chocolate has melted and the drink is hot. Stir in the kahlua, if using. Ladle into cups and top with a few mini marshmallows.

Ways to cheat

In an ideal world we would all like to make supper from scratch every day, but most of us just don't have the time. The recipes in this chapter include some easy shortcuts using storecupboard ingredients combined with a few ready-made sauces and chilled convenience foods.

PREPARATION TIME **15 minutes**

COOKING TEMPERATURE **low**

COOKING TIME **6–7 hours**

SERVES **4**

$\mathscr{M}$eatballs & tagliatelle

1 tablespoon olive oil

2 x 350 g (11½ oz) packs of 12 beef meatballs

1 onion, chopped

400 g (13 oz) jar roasted vegetable and tomato pasta sauce

200 ml (7 fl oz) red wine

375 g (12 oz) tagliatelle

small bunch of basil (optional)

chunk of Parmesan cheese, grated or shaved, to serve

Preheat the slow cooker if necessary; see the manufacturer's handbook. Heat the oil in a large frying pan, add the meatballs and fry, in batches if necessary, until browned but not cooked through. Scoop out of the pan with a slotted spoon and transfer to the slow cooker pot.

Add the onion to the frying pan and fry, stirring, for 5 minutes or until softened. Drain off most of the fat, then pour in the pasta sauce and red wine. Bring the mixture to the boil, stirring, then pour over the meatballs.

Cover with the lid and cook on low for 6–7 hours. Just before serving put the pasta in a large saucepan of boiling water and cook for 9–10 minutes until just tender. Drain in a colander.

Tear the basil leaves, if using, over the meatballs in the slow cooker, add the drained pasta and toss together. Spoon into shallow bowls and serve sprinkled with some grated or shaved Parmesan.

Ready-made meatballs are an excellent secret ingredient. Mix any jar of pasta sauce, some red wine and basil and you can create an easy supper that is smart enough to serve to friends. If you are making this for children use beef stock instead of the wine.

Chicken with thyme
& mushroom sauce

25 g (1 oz) butter

1 tablespoon olive oil

4 boneless, skinless chicken breasts, about 625 g (1¼ lb) in total

1 small onion, thinly sliced

200 g (7 oz) closed-cup mushrooms, sliced

415 g (13½ oz) can cream of chicken soup

2 tablespoons sherry

1–2 sprigs of thyme

TO SERVE

new potatoes

broccoli

Preheat the slow cooker if necessary; see the manufacturer's handbook. Heat half the butter and the oil in a frying pan, add the chicken breasts and fry briefly until browned on both sides. Lift out of the pan with a slotted spoon and transfer to the slow cooker pot.

Add the onion to the pan and fry, stirring, for 5 minutes or until softened. Add the remaining butter and the mushrooms and fry for 2–3 minutes.

Pour in the soup and sherry and bring to the boil. Add the thyme to the slow cooker pot and pour the soup mixture over the top.

Cover with the lid and cook on low for 7–8 hours or until the chicken is tender. Test by inserting a small knife into the centre of one of the breasts in the centre of the pot; if the juices run clear they are ready. Spoon on to plates, discard the thyme and serve with new potatoes and steamed broccoli.

A can of soup can be used as a substitute for a homemade sauce. Chicken soup has been used in this recipe, but you could use tomato, mixed vegetable or mushroom.

PREPARATION TIME **10 minutes**

COOKING TEMPERATURE **low and high**

COOKING TIME **8½–10½ hours**

SERVES **4**

$\mathscr{L}$amb stew
with dumplings

1 tablespoon sunflower oil

625 g (1¼ lb) lamb rump or chump steaks

1 leek, sliced; white and green parts kept separate

2 carrots, diced

2 x 415 g (13½ oz) cans Scotch broth

180 g (6¼ oz) pack herby dumpling mix

5–6 tablespoons water

Preheat the slow cooker if necessary; see the manufacturer's handbook. Heat the oil in a frying pan, add the lamb and fry until browned on both sides. Lift out with a slotted spoon and transfer to the slow cooker pot.

Add the white leek slices to the frying pan and cook for 2–3 minutes until just softened. Add the carrots and cans of soup, bring to the boil, stirring, then pour over the lamb. Cover with the lid and cook on low for 8–10 hours.

When almost ready to serve, tip the dumpling mix into a bowl. Using a fork, gradually mix in enough water to make a soft but not sticky dough. Divide into 8 and roll each piece into a ball.

Stir the green leek slices into the casserole, arrange the dumplings on top, replace the lid and cook on high for 30 minutes until the dumplings are well risen and the tops are dry. Spoon the stew and dumplings into shallow bowls to serve.

Lamb rump or chump chops have been used in this recipe for speed, but if you prefer you could buy shoulder steaks or lamb fillet and slice or dice it before frying.

PREPARATION TIME **15 minutes**

COOKING TEMPERATURE **low**

COOKING TIME **8–9 hours**

SERVES **4**

Chinese spiced beef

2 tablespoon sunflower oil

750 g (1½ lb) ready-diced
    stewing beef

1 onion, thinly sliced

2.5 cm (1 inch) fresh root ginger,
    peeled and finely chopped

425 g (14 oz) jar hoisin and five
    spice cook-in sauce

270 g (8½ oz) pack ready-prepared
    stir-fry vegetable mix

2 spring onions, thinly sliced

385 g (12½ oz) pack chilled
    egg noodles

small bunch of coriander

Preheat the slow cooker if necessary; see the manufacturer's handbook. Heat 1 tablespoon oil in a frying pan, add the beef, a few pieces at a time, until all the pieces are in the pan, then fry, stirring, until browned all over. Scoop the meat out of the pan with a slotted spoon and transfer it to the slow cooker pot.

Add the onion to the pan and fry, stirring, for 5 minutes or until it is just beginning to brown. Stir in the ginger, then add the jar of cook-in sauce. Bring to the boil, stirring, then pour into the slow cooker pot. Cover with the lid and cook on low for 8–9 hours until the beef is tender.

When almost ready to serve, heat the remaining oil in a clean frying pan, add the stir-fry mix and spring onions and cook for 3–4 minutes until just beginning to soften. Push the vegetables to one side of the pan. Add the noodles and cook for 2–3 minutes until hot.

Spoon the noodles into shallow bowls, stir the beef and spoon on top. Serve sprinkled with the vegetables and torn coriander leaves.

Use this recipe as a basis and adapt it as you wish, adding other flavoured ready-made sauces. There should be enough liquid to just cover the meat, but if there is not add a little extra boiling water or a splash of wine or cider.

Cauliflower & spinach balti

1 tablespoon sunflower oil

1 onion, chopped

540 g (1 lb 3 oz) can balti curry sauce

1 large cauliflower, core discarded and florets cut into large pieces (about 750 g (1½ lb) prepared weight)

410 g (13½ oz) green lentils, drained

150 g (5 oz) spinach, washed and torn into pieces

naan bread, to serve

Preheat the slow cooker if necessary; see the manufacturer's handbook. Heat the oil in a frying pan, add the onion and fry, stirring, for 5 minutes or until softened. Add the curry sauce and bring to the boil.

Add the cauliflower and lentils to the slow cooker pot. Pour over the hot sauce, cover with the lid and cook on low for 5–6 hours or until the cauliflower is tender.

Stir the cauliflower and sprinkle the spinach on top. Replace the lid and cook, still on low, for 10–15 minutes until the spinach is just wilted. Spoon into bowls and serve with warm naan bread.

The amount of liquid and size of vegetable chunk greatly affects the speed of cooking in a slow cooker. The more liquid there is and the smaller the size of the vegetable chunks, the quicker the cooking.

*M*editerranean
shepherd's pie

2 tablespoons olive oil

1 onion, chopped

1 aubergine, diced

500 g (1 lb) minced lamb

2 garlic cloves, finely chopped

400 g (13 oz) jar tomato pasta sauce

1 courgette, diced

850 g (1 lb 10 oz) pack chilled
  ready-made mashed potato

4 tablespoons freshly grated
  Parmesan or Cheddar cheese

Preheat the slow cooker if necessary; see the manufacturer's handbook. Heat the oil in a frying pan, add the onion and aubergine and fry for 5 minutes, stirring until softened. Scoop the mixture out of the pan with a slotted spoon and transfer to the slow cooker pot.

Add the lamb to the frying pan and dry-fry, stirring, for 5 minutes until browned. Add the garlic and pasta sauce and bring to the boil, stirring.

Add the courgette to the slow cooker pot and pour the sauce over the top. Cover and cook on low for 8–10 hours.

When almost ready to serve, microwave the mashed potato, following the instructions on the packet. Stir the mash and stir the mince with separate spoons, then spoon the potato over the top of the mince. Sprinkle with grated cheese, then lift the slow cooker pot out of the machine housing with oven gloves. Brown the pie under a preheated hot grill and serve with peas.

Chocolate croissant
& pecan pudding

50 g (2 oz) butter

4 chocolate croissants

50 g (2 oz) caster sugar

¼ teaspoon ground cinnamon

40 g (1½ oz) pecan nuts, roughly
  crushed

300 ml (½ pint) full-fat milk

2 whole eggs

2 egg yolks

1 teaspoon vanilla extract

cream, to serve

Grease the inside of a 1.2 litre (2 pint) straight-sided ovenproof dish with a little of the butter (checking first that the dish will fit into your slow cooker).

Thickly slice the croissants and spread one side of each slice with the remaining butter. Mix together the sugar and spice. Arrange the croissants in layers in the dish, sprinkling each layer with the spiced sugar and the pecans.

Whisk the milk, eggs and egg yolks with the vanilla extract. Pour into the dish and leave to soak for 15 minutes. Preheat the slow cooker if necessary; see the manufacturer's handbook.

Loosely cover the top of the pudding with buttered foil, then lower it into the slow cooker pot. Pour boiling water into the pot to come halfway up the sides of the dish, cover with the lid and cook on low for 4–4½ hours or until the custard is set and the pudding well risen.

Lift the dish out of the slow cooker with oven gloves. Scoop into bowls and serve with cream.

For a more traditional bread and butter pudding, use 4 slices of buttered bread and sprinkle the layers with sugar and a few spoonfuls of dried fruit instead of the cinnamon and pecans. Make up the custard with vanilla extract.

Cherry & coconut
sponge pudding

butter, for greasing

40 g (1½ oz) desiccated coconut

400 g (13 oz) can cherry pie filling

500 g (1 lb) pack Madeira cake mix

4 tablespoons sunflower oil or 1 egg
  (see cake mix instructions)

vanilla ice cream, to serve (optional)

Preheat the slow cooker if necessary; see the manufacturer's handbook. Lightly butter a 1.5 litre (2½ pint) pudding basin and line the base with a circle of greaseproof or nonstick baking paper. Sprinkle in a little of the coconut, then tilt and turn the basin until the buttery sides are lightly coated. Spoon half the cherry pie filling into the bottom of the basin.

Tip the cake mix into a bowl and mix in the oil or egg and water as the instructions on the pack direct.

Stir in the remaining coconut, then spoon into the basin and level the surface. Cover the top with a piece of buttered foil, making a fold in the centre, or doming up the top slightly, to allow the pudding to rise. Tie the foil in place with string and lower the basin into the slow cooker pot.

Pour boiling water into the slow cooker pot to come halfway up the sides of the basin, cover with the lid and cook on high for 3–3½ hours or until the sponge is well risen, feels dry and springs back when pressed with a fingertip.

Remove the basin from the slow cooker pot with oven gloves and loosen the edge of the pudding with a round-bladed knife. Turn out on to a plate, remove the basin and peel away the lining paper. Warm the remaining pie filling in a microproof bowl in a microwave for 45–60 seconds on full power until hot. Serve the pudding with the remaining cherries and scoops of vanilla ice cream, if liked.

Mix and match your own flavour combinations by using a chocolate cake mix or a can of apple pie filling livened up with some grated lemon or orange rind.

$\mathscr{R}$aspberry & rhubarb
oaty crumble

400 g (13 oz) trimmed rhubarb

150 g (5 oz) frozen raspberries

50 g (2 oz) caster sugar

3 tablespoons water

thick cream, to serve

TOPPING

15 g (¹/₂ oz) butter

3 tablespoons flaked almonds

200 g (7 oz), about 4, ready-made flapjacks

Preheat the slow cooker if necessary; see the manufacturer's handbook. Cut the rhubarb into 2.5 cm (1 inch) thick slices and add to the slow cooker pot with the still-frozen raspberries, the sugar and water.

Cover with the lid and cook on low for 2–3 hours until the rhubarb is just tender.

When almost ready to serve, heat the butter in a frying pan, add the almonds and crumble in the flapjacks. Fry, stirring, for 3–4 minutes until hot and lightly browned.

Spoon the fruit into bowls, sprinkle the crumble over the top and serve with thick cream.

$\mathcal{T}$offee apple pancakes

50 g (2 oz) butter

75 g (3 oz) light muscovado sugar

2 tablespoons golden syrup

4 dessert apples, cored and each cut into 8 slices

juice of 1 lemon

375 g (12 oz) pack or 6 chilled or long-life pancakes

grated chocolate, to decorate (optional)

vanilla ice cream, to serve

Preheat the slow cooker if necessary; see the manufacturer's handbook. Heat the butter, sugar and syrup in a microproof bowl in a microwave for 1–1½ minutes on full power until the butter has just melted.

Add the apples and lemon juice to the slow cooker pot and toss together. Stir the butter mix and pour it over the apple. Cover with the lid and cook on high for 1–1½ hours.

Heat the pancakes in a microwave according to the instructions on the back of the pack. Fold in half and arrange on serving plates. Stir the apple mix, then spoon it on to the pancakes. Top with a scoop of vanilla ice cream and sprinkle with a little grated chocolate, if liked.

For those of you who really like chocolate, coat the pancakes with a little chocolate spread before microwaving, and then top with the apples and toffee sauce.

Index

Acknowledgements

Executive Editor Eleanor Maxfield

Senior Editor Charlotte Macey

Executive Art Editor Penny Stock

Designer Barbara Zuñiga

Senior Production Controller Amanda Mackie

Photographer Stephen Conroy

Food Stylist Sara Lewis

Props Stylist Liz Hippisley

Special Photography: © Octopus Publishing Group Limited/Stephen Conroy